ZAKYNTHOS

the flower of the Levant

EDITIONS
TOUBI'S
ΕΚΔΟΣΕΙΣ

ATHENS 1999

Texts: J. SOLMAN, ANG. VIVARDIS, G. VOYIATZIS, D. THEODORAKATOS
Editor (greek text): DAPHNE CHRISTOU
Collaborating Experts: A. VLACHOUTSIKOU - D.C. MENCHERO (biologists), N. TSELEPIDIS (geologist)

Photographs: DORA KOLIOPANOU, TAKIS SPYROPOULOS, M. TOUBIS ARCHIVE

Design: ANGELA SGOUROU
Typesetting, colour separations, montage, printing: M. TOUBIS GRAPHIC ARTS S.A.

Copyright © 1999 MICHALIS TOUBIS PUBLICATIONS S.A.
Vouliagmenis Ave. 519, Ilioupoli, 163 41, Athens Tel: (01) 9923876, Fax: 9923867

INTERNET: http://www.toubis.gr

ISBN: 960-540-356-0

We wish to thank Mr. N. Lykouresis for his contribution to the publication of this book.
We also thank the Sarakinado Association for the photograhs they made available,
Mr. A. Milanos, president of the Naval Museum and Mrs St. Gasparatou,
responsible for the public relations of such museum, whose contribution also proved valuable.

O beloved homeland
O wonderful island
Zakynthos: you have given me
the spirit and the gifts
of Apollo

from the poem "THE PATRIOT"
A. KALVOS

CONTENTS

CONTENTS

1 ZAKYNTHOS

Zakynthos, the celebrated island in the Ionian sea, has been praised by both Greek and foreign travellers. It has been described as an earthly paradise, a floating garden, and a poetic nymph. And justifiably so. The gentle landscape with its rocky eminencies creates an illusion of a paradise on earth, a source of inspiration for all kinds of crea-

tivity. Zakynthos, the island that took its name from the most beautiful of flowers, as Poe put it, captivates you with the huge numbers of wild flowers you see on its green plain, and the jasmine in the courtyards of the houses.
It captivates you with its clear, pellucid waters and superb beaches. You could believe that

the flower of the Levant

Artemis is still roaming its shady forests, and the melodies from the lyre of Apollo, god of music and light, become echoes of ages past. It is no coincidence that on Zakynthos, the poetry of nature gave way so generously to the poetry of life, and of the art that gives expression to it, for here art and nature come together in harmonious pairing. Home of Greek civilisation, of the Greek poets Andreas Kalvos and Dionysios Solomos, and the playwright Grigorios Xenopoulos, the island always enjoyed a high level of cultural activity, which continues down to the present.

The town of Zakynthos in an engraving of 1834.

Here Venetian influence was kneaded with the Greek tradition to produce a distinctive culture of delicate tones, every manifestation of which is graceful.

Theatre flourished on the island from the 15th century onwards, while music, responding to the teachings of Apollo, attained its finest and most representative creation in the Zakynthian serenades sung by Zakynthians beneath the window of their loved one, in an age when Shakespearean love was not a cinematic affair but an intense moment of life itself. On Zakynthos, people have music in their veins, and musicality is part of their lives. As exponents of an advanced culture, they have learned to find beauty even amidst the ruins of destruction. They have long shown great sensitivity to the protection of the natural environment, and of the various rare species of the marine ecosystem. The beautiful natural environment is in any event the attraction that brings large numbers of visitors here every year. The superb beaches with their crystal-clear sea sometimes stand out against a virgin natural landscape, and sometimes lie hidden beneath the shade of caves, where they can be detected only by the experienced eye.

Zakynthos is a beautiful, verdant island, and its inhabitants are descendants of an advanced civilisation.

At this spot in the Ionian sea, memory recalls older, loved functions and life finds its familiar rhythms. The Greek poet Andreas Kalvos fittingly described the island:

"Beautiful and solitary
Zakynthos has conquered me!"

Nature is full of surprises on Zakynthos.

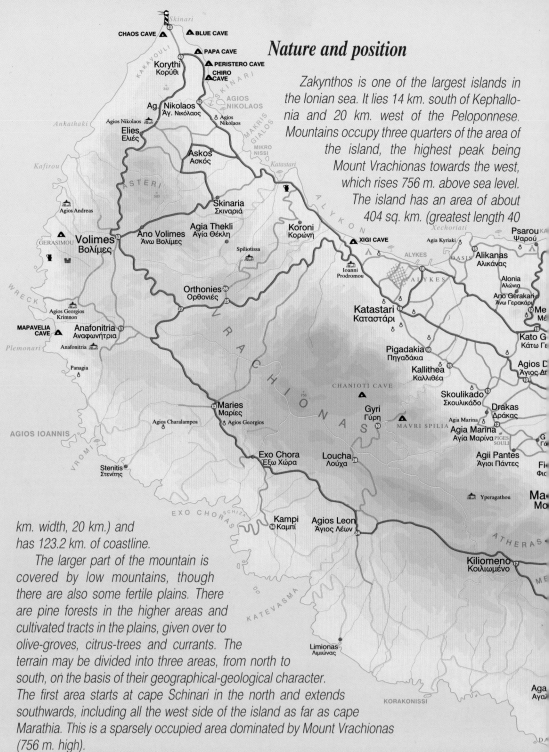

Nature and position

Zakynthos is one of the largest islands in the Ionian sea. It lies 14 km. south of Kephallonia and 20 km. west of the Peloponnese. Mountains occupy three quarters of the area of the island, the highest peak being Mount Vrachionas towards the west, which rises 756 m. above sea level. The island has an area of about 404 sq. km. (greatest length 40 km. width, 20 km.) and has 123.2 km. of coastline.

The larger part of the mountain is covered by low mountains, though there are also some fertile plains. There are pine forests in the higher areas and cultivated tracts in the plains, given over to olive-groves, citrus-trees and currants. The terrain may be divided into three areas, from north to south, on the basis of their geographical-geological character. The first area starts at cape Schinari in the north and extends southwards, including all the west side of the island as far as cape Marathia. This is a sparsely occupied area dominated by Mount Vrachionas (756 m. high).

The central area, which starts at the bay of Alykes in the north and ends at Laganas bay, includes the fertile plain and the town of Zakynthos. It is a plain region with fertile soil, and it is here that the majority of the roughly 35,000 inhabitants of the island live. The third area includes the east and south-east side of the island as far as cape Yeraki, and is dominated by Mount Skopos (492 m.).

There are no rivers on the island, just a few winter torrents. The west part is occupied by bare mountain peaks and steep cliffs, which plunge abruptly down to the sea. The main plateaux, which are still cultivated today, are Volima (420 m.) in the north part, Yiri (550 m.) in the centre of the island, Aghios Leon (380 m.) in the south part, and finally the plateau at Agalas (290 m.).

The entire mountainous west part of the island is dry and arid and is accordingly sparsely populated. There is also a distinct vertical division of the island, about a line running NNE-SSW, with high mountains to the west (Kaki Rachi 680 m., Vouno 553 m, Megalo Vouno 605 m., Psili Rachi 447 m. etc.). In contrast, the smaller, east part consists of plains, in which there are many natural springs and considerable vegetation. The larger part of the population lives in this part of the island, in which lies the town of Zakynthos. The west part of the island is poor in socio-economic terms, with only a small number of villages, whereas the east part, with its plains, has luxuriant vegetation, a mild climate in which olives, currents, citrus fruit, etc. prosper, and a large number of villages and farm houses.

Zakynthos has a mild, Mediterranean climate, and is a good holiday centre all the year round. In August the climate is dry and cool, with average temperatures reaching 27°. The north and north-west, humid, winds that blow bring considerable rainfall to the island, thanks to which it has lavish greenery and many natural springs. Snow rarely falls on Zakynthos.

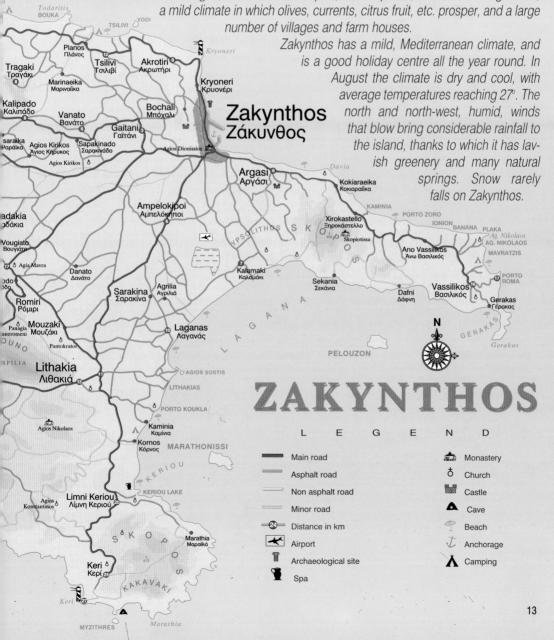

ZAKYNTHOS

L E G E N D

Main road	Monastery
Asphalt road	Church
Non asphalt road	Castle
Minor road	Cave
Distance in km	Beach
Airport	Anchorage
Archaeological site	Camping
Spa	

Geology

Geologically speaking, most of Zakynthos is part of the Paxoi zone, with only the south-east end (Mount Skopos) belonging to the Ionian zone. The two zones are tectonic plates, and the Paxoi plate is being subducted beneath the Ionian plate. The subduction front runs NNE-SSW. The Paxos zone occupies all the rest of the island.

The Ionian zone is represented by sediments of the Triassic period (about 235 to 209 million years ago), consisting of varieties of gypsum, which are disturbed on account of breaks. It also includes black, fine-grained plakodeis, strongly vitroumeniouchous limestone, known as limestone with cardita. This entire zone is confined to Skopos. The Paxoi zone is composed of the following minerals and rocks (from the earliest to the most recent): white, stratified classic limestone containing fossils (Upper Cretaceous: 85 x 65 million years ago). These are followed by shallow-sea limestone containing coral (Eocene-Oligocene (56 to 23 million years). Finally, sandstone, [ilioliths and marges], with the upper strata containing layers of gypsum and synectic argil. The most recent sedimentary rocks in the Paxoi zone are of Miocene date (23 to 8 million years).

The rock formations in both zones are in places covered by more recent sediments, of Pliocene, Pleistocene and Oligocene date. Most of them are found mainly in the east part of the island and overlie sediments in the Ionian zone.

The most recent rocks result from the sedimentation of a variety of material deposited in low-lying regions. Amidst areas of dolines and polges, mainly in small mountain plateaux, can be found gomosis material such as red marges (clay and sandy clay containing red soil). On the steep coasts, contemporary coastal deposits can be also found.

Finally, we may note the medicinal sulphur springs at Tetartia (Yerakari), Kalosourtis (Alykes bay), Vromoneri, Paleochora and Xyngia.

Agriculture map of Zakynthos.

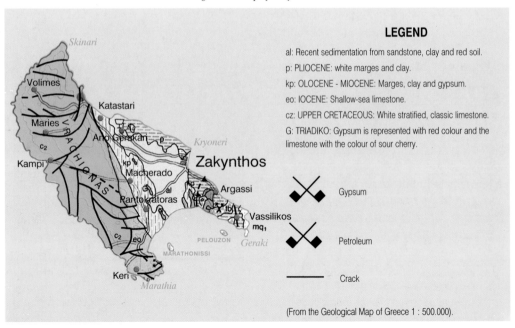

LEGEND

al: Recent sedimentation from sandstone, clay and red soil.

p: PLIOCENE: white marges and clay.

kp: OLOCENE - MIOCENE: Marges, clay and gypsum.

eo: IOCENE: Shallow-sea limestone.

cz: UPPER CRETACEOUS: White stratified, classic limestone.

G: TRIADIKO: Gypsum is represented with red colour and the limestone with the colour of sour cherry.

Gypsum

Petroleum

Crack

(From the Geological Map of Greece 1 : 500.000).

Geomorphology

The present geomorphology of Zakynthos is the product of plate tectonics, the mineral composition of the island, and its climate. Its main feature is an asymmetrical anticline running NNE-SSW. The creation, breaching and subsequent erosion of this has created four geomorphological areas:

A) **West mountainous limestone mass.** This area is rocky and extends from Keri to cape Schinari. Its main feature is the presence of limestone and its sharp, relief landscape. The general orientation of the geomorphological axes here is NW-SE. In the broader area, there are dimiourgia dolinon and large carstic depressions, including the creation of caves (Koukezi).

B) **South-east mountainous area of Skopos.** This includes the Skopos peninsula, and is built of gypsum and limestone. Here, too, there is a sharp relief landscape, and the geomorphological axes extend NE-SW.

C) **East hilly region.** The hilly region extends to the fringes of the mountain masses, and to the ESE part of the island. These hills consist mainly of argils and marges The larger part of the plain is covered by modern deposits. The present winter torrents are corroding earlier geological formations and deposit their sediment on the coasts (sand, pebbles, etc). There are a number of natural springs in this area.

D) **Plains area – depression.** This is located in the central-eastern part of the island and consists of fertile terrain, created by the decomposition of the minerals in the surrounding alluvial basin. The basin was created as a result of the rixigeni tectonics of the area, with a system of fissures oriented NNW-SSE. The horizontal fragmentation of the island is quite pronounced, particularly on the west side, where there are many bays, coves, capes and small headlands. There is also a distinct vertical fragmentation, with high mountains. The hydrographic network is very dense, apart from the plains area, through which flow three seasonal torrents that issue into the bays of Zakynthos, Lagana and Alykes.

Flora and fauna

Zakynthos has five types of vegetation, comprising different groups of plants. On the south and east coast are sandy areas with typical coastal vegetation. Here, amongst the ammothines, can be found the rare sea lily pancratium maritimum.

In the west there are steep, rocky areas in which native species are to be found, amongst which are asperula naufraga and stachys iconica. The former of these is a very rare species found only on Zakynthos, and in the case of the latter, Zakynthos is the southernmost point at which it occurs. Another plant native to Zakynthos, the limonium zacynthium, can be found on the islets in the Bay of Laganas.

A large part of the island is covered with bushes and shrubs, which have spread to areas burnt by forest fires in the past. We may note at this point the existence of a small shrub hypericum aegypticum, which is common on Zakynthos but rare in the rest of Greece.

The fourth type of vegetation on the island occurs in the pine forests. In these forest grows the beautiful peony paeonia mascula, which is becoming increasingly rare through being plucked.

Hygrophilous vegetation is found in the many irrigation canals dug in the plains of Zakynthos, and around the airport, where there was once a lake, and also in Lake Keri. Here you will find the rare orchid orchis palustris, which is in danger of becoming extinct on the island as a result of the deterioration of the lake and of being plucked by ill-informed visitors.

The bird-life on Zakynthos is also of some interest, due to the fact that the island is an important resting-place for migratory birds on their journey to and from Africa. Many species of sparrow-forms can be seen, mainly in the olive-groves of Zakynthos, which also abound in owls (athne noctua).

The wetlands on the island at Lake Keri and Alykes are visited seasonally by various species of erodion, such as the stachtotsiknia (ardea cinerea), the egret (egretta garzetta), and the night-crow (nicticorax nicticorax), a erodios that also fishes at night. Swans and pelicans have also been observed in this area.

The cliffs of the west coast are home to the petritis falco peregrinus), mavropetrites (falco eleonorae), cormorant (phalacrocorax carbo), sea cormorant (phalorocorax aristotelis) and asi-moglaros. Although land mammals are now rare on Zakynthos, due to the use of anti-rodent poisons, one can still see hedgehogs (erinaceus concolor) and martens (martes foina).

Various species of dolphin, such as rinodel-phini (tursiops truncatus), zonodelphini (stenella coeruleoalba), and stactodelphini (grampus griseus), can be seen, and large cetaceans such as ziphius cavirostris and physeter macro-cephalus have been observed off Zakynthus and in the bay of Laganas. The Mediterranean seal (Monachus monachus) is found all around the island; because of its rarity the discussion of this animal merits a special chapter.

Protected species

Zakynthos plays host to two endangered species of vertebrates, the Mediterranean seal Monachus monacus and the sea turtle Caretta caretta. Both these species, and their biotopes are protected by international and Greek legislation. The seal lives on the rocky coasts of the island, where it bears its young. Visits to the caves in which they rest disturbs the seals and create a serious problem for this species, so it is important when visiting the coasts of the island on a guided excursion to make sure that the boat respects the legislation in force forbidding the disturbance of these seals in the caves that are their habitat.

The famous Mediterranean turtle Caretta caretta, which for millions of years has used the south coasts of Zakynthos for reproduction, finds a safe haven on protected beaches.

Caretta caretta was once abundant throughout the entire Mediterranean, but human intervention and the thoughtless exploitation of the natural environment have reduced its numbers to the point where the species is now threatened with extinction. It is therefore very important to protect the areas in which it reproduces, such as the coasts of Zakynthos.

The beaches of Zakynthos are not only beautiful, but contribute to the ecological balance of the planet.

The Mediterranean Society for the Preservation of the Sea Turtle (MEDASSET) is an international, non-governmental organisation founded in England in 1988, the aim of which is to preserve the sea turtles of the Mediterranean. Since 1997, MEDASSET has collaborated with the Anton Dohn Research Centre for Zoology and the Care of Sea Turtles in Naples, Italy to carry out a programme of satellite monitoring of sea turtle migration.

As part of this programme, a Caretta caretta turtle, called "Paola", had a transmitter attached to it which relayed its position to a satellite after the turtle was released from the Skala beach on Kephallonia. Alongside its other activities, MEDASSET has inaugurated a public information programme concerning litter and its impact on the marine environment.

Special kiosks have been set up at Laganas and Yerakas to provide information on the turtles and the ways in which we can help them. More specifically:

We can contribute to the protection of the most important biotope of Caretta caretta in the Mediterranean, by signing a document calling for the creation of a National Marine Park of Zakynthos. The purpose of this Park is the effective protection of the turtles and the coasts that are their habitat, and to establish links with the local community.

The creation of this National Marine Park and its promotion at international level will result in the upgrading of tourism to Zakynthos and bring long-term benefits to all the inhabitants of the island.

Sea turtle Caretta caretta and Mediterranean seal Monachus monachus are protected species.

List of guidelines to visitors issued by title, MEDASSET:

- It is strictly forbidden to stay on the beach after sunset. The turtles emerge from the sea to lay their eggs during hours of darkness.

- Do not dig in the sand, especially in the upper part of the beach.

- Do not use sunshades that have to be stuck in the sand. Sunshades will probably destroy nests, because their shade reduces the temperature of the sand, thus modifying the conditions under which the eggs are hatched.

- Do not bring vehicles on to the beach, and do not let dogs dig in the sand. At the beginning of summer, when the turtles come out of the sea to make their nests, they leave tracks in the sand made by their fins as they try to drag their heavy bodies up the beach and back again to the sea. Beach games should therefore be avoided, since they may uncover a nest, and holes in the sand often become death traps for the baby turtles as they try to make their way to the sea.

- It is forbidden to use lights that reflect on the sea. Urge the owners of houses, hotels and shops to cover or lower their lights near beaches were eggs are laid.

- It is forbidden to take baby turtles away, or to help them find their way to the sea. It is essential that the newly born turtles should rely exclusively on their own efforts to find the sea, however harsh this may seem.

MYTH & HISTORY

From ancient times to modern period

Myths & Prehistory

It tells of how Artemis, goddess of wild life and virgin huntress, loved roaming the rich forest of Zakynthos, while her brother Apollo, god of light and music but also of archery, was equally charmed by the island and sat among the laurel trees with his followers, playing the lyre. One of these traditional accounts mentioned also by Homer, tells of Zakynthos, son of Dardanos, arriving with men and ships from the Arcadian town of Psophida, building and fortifying an acropolis. According to Pliny the island was called Hyria, after an earlier founder, the hero Hyrieus from Arcadia.

Plan of Zakynthos.

Although the ancient writers attest that Zakynthos was inhabited during the fifteenth and sixteenth centuries BC - Thucydides mentions that the first settlers were Achaians from the Peloponnese. Other versions of prehistoric times have been formulated, which bring us up to 10th century BC. When the Arcadian settlers arrived in the island, they built fortifications and prospered sufficiently to be able to send out colonists of their own. Their ships took them to the shores of Spain, where they founded a daughter city, which they called Zakantha. This became a flourishing commercial and cultural town, which prospered for more than a thousand years. In 218 BC it was besieged by Hannibal.

Other settlers from Zakynthos founded the town of Kidonies on Crete, a colony on Paros island and, jointly with the Phocaeans, the town of Phokida (or Parnassia) on the Pyerenean headland in Spain. Later on the prehistoric period, Zakynthos was successively ruled by Arkeisios, king of Kephalonia, by Laertis and Laertis' son Odysseus, Homer's king of Ithaca. Odysseus' people - from Ithaki, Kephalonia, Lefkada and Akarnania - sent a total of twelve ships to the war with Troy, and Homer in the Iliad is not sparing with his praises of their courage. He refers to them under the general name of "Kephalines" After the end of the Trojan War and when Odysseus has finally returned to Ithaca, Homer tells of the destruction by Odysseus of his wife Penelope's importunate mentions the killing of twenty young men from Zakynthos. It seems that Homer's tale of the suitors reflects what was in fact a revolt of the islands, which resulted in the end of Odysseus' rule over them. Neoptolemus was the intermediary who organised the signing of a treaty giving the islands their independence in return for an annual tribute tax. The Neoptolemus treaty was the first such in Greek history which established the independence of a country and provided for its democratic rule.

Vase-painting with a scene of Odysseus killing the suitors (5th century BC).

Historical period

Zakynthos played no significant role in antiquity, despite the fact that it was a rich and commercially prosperous island. It owed its commercial development to its geographical locations and to its bitumen springs. Silver coins minted in the 6th century AD depicting the sacred symbol of the trident indicate that the islanders worshipped the cult of Apollo. During the Peloponnesian War Zakynthos fought on the side of the Athenians. When the Lacedaemonians had recovered from the early defects in deflected on their naval forces by Athens and had begun to built up a proper fleet, they send the Spartan general Knymos with a hundred ships to conquer Zakynthos in 430 BC. Next the Zakynthians are known to have sent ships with the Sicilian campaign in 415 BC, which ended with the crushing defeat of the Athenians in 413. The Athenian alliance fell apart shortly afterwards, and Zakynthos once more found itself under Lacedaemonian domination. It even exchanged its democratic constitution for an oligarchic one. During the Macedonian wars, Zakynthos tried again to remain neutral, just as it had done in the Persian Wars. It did not succeed. The island fell first to the Macedonians, the to the Romans, and then again to the Macedonians, who eventually gave Zakynthos to King Aminandras.

1. Stater of Zakynthos (5th century BC).
2. Roman coin of Zakynthos (2nd century AD).

Roman Period

From the moment the first Roman occupation of the island ended, Rome tried hard to get Zakynthos back, appreciating not only its geographical advantages for commerce and conquests, but also its inherent wealth and the capabilities of its people. This did not, however, please the people of Zakynthos, and they organised in insurrection. The outraged Romans promptly dispatched a naval force to teach the islanders a lesson. They burned and destroyed whatever they could, and posted a garrison on Zakynthos. The Zakynthians with the help of Aetolians drove the Roman garrison off the island again. The Roman reaction was swift. They sent off their general Fulvius, who vanquished the Aetolians and reconquered Zakynthos in 150 BC. Fulvius strategy seems to have borne fruit, and the Roman overlords and the local population learnt to live with each other in mutual give and take. Later general Mithridate Archelaos was sent to take Zakynthos. On this occasion the islanders fought stoutly at the side of the Roman soldiers, and Archelaos had finally to call off the siege of Zakynthos and sail off home in 87 BC without having achieved his purpose. After separation Roman provinces, Zakynthos began to concern to province of Achaia. It is period of an autonomy of an island, which was considerably advanced and was regularly visited by known philosophers of Rome.

Byzantine Period

The decline and fall of the Roman Empire gave a fresh impetus to the pirates and to other would-be conquerors, who all renewed their attacks on Zakynthos and the other Eptanissos islands of the Ionian and the western Mediterranean generally. When Constantine the Great founded the Byzantine Empire, Zakynthos became part of the province of Illyria. After Constantine's death his squabbling successors neglected the outlying parts of the empire, and the raids and the plundering resumed in full force.

In terms of social organisation in the Byzantine era, the people of Zakynthos belonged to one of three classes. In the top calls were the epiphanies, the big landowners of the island, the second class was comprised of artisans and merchants, and the third calls consisted of farmers. Christianity came to Zakynthos early. There is a local tradition that in 34 AD Mary Magdalene came to the island en route from Jerusalem to Rome, and her ship anchored for a while on the western coast of Zakynthos where she preached the teachings of Jesus Nazareth.

Memories of the Byzantine culture of Zakynthos are revived in the Byzantine Museum.

Zakynthos suffered extensive destruction in 466 AD, when the African Vandal King Gizarich arrived with sixty ships and his pen fell to plunder, rape and slaughter, and set fire to Zakynthos town. When Gizerich left, he took with him five hundred of the "upper crust" landowners, whom he butchered as his ships sailed out into the Adriatic and flung their bodies overboard.

One characteristic of Byzantine Zakynthos, however, is the continuity of Western influence in its administration in contrast to the rest of Greece. The island belonged to Rome until the 8th century AD. The years that followed brought new pirate raids, by the Saracens this time, and new catastrophes. In 844 Byzantium sent out its commander Nikitas, and later on his deputy Nassar. Around this time Zakynthos and Cephalonia were taken out of the province of Achaia and placed in the 11th district of Longovarda. Later still, a specifically Byzantine district of Cephalonia was formed, which included all the seven Ionian islets.

The Crusaders and Frankish Rule (1185 - 1485)

By the time the Byzantine Empire was drawing to its close, the appetite of the European aristocracy for conquests in eastern lands had been growing rapidly, fed by unceasingly ambitious ruthlessness. Under the pretext of liberating the Holy Land from the heathens, crusader's armies of adventurers and booty-hunters swarmed to invade the riches of the East. On the way home from one such crusade, the Norman noble Voimonde fell with insane fury on the Eptanissos islands, intent on revenging the failure of his father Giscard to take Zakynthos and Cephalonia to 1084.

In 1147 the Normans came again, led by Rogiro I, and occupied all the Ionian isles. Although Emperor Emanuel of Byzantium managed with the help of the Venetians to take the islands back, he was eventually forced to sign a peace treaty with Rigiro in 1158. In 1185 Zakynthos and Cephalonia broke away finally from the Byzantine Empire. They formed the palatinate of

Cephalonia and Zakynthos, which was maintained for three whole centuries, until 1479, initially under the rule, or overlord ship of the Orsini family, then the Angenins, and subsequently by Tocci and his descendants. The need to remain on favour with Rome and its papal rulers, who could guarantee their protection, pushed the Orsinis into forcing Catholicism on the islanders and doing away with the Bishoprics on Zakynthos and Cephalonia. In 1335, the Orsini line came to an end.

In 1357 the island passed to the Tocco dynasty, which ruled it for over a century. The new rulers, equally ambitious but more capable than their predecessors succeeded in increasing the possessions of the palatinate, seizing lands in Epirus (on the Greek mainland). At the same time, they managed to organise the administration and finances of the island, bestowing on the region a period of peace and stability. Leonardo I did what could to further the overall development of the Ionian islands, and set them firmly on the road to progress and prosperity. Most of his work was undone again by his successor, Carlos I, who was a selfish leader, unloved by the people, insatiable, violent and ever looking for war. Carlos I died in Ioannina in 1429, and appointed as his successor his nephew Carlos II. His successor, Leonardo III, and unstable opportunist, kept fighting the Turks - sometimes winning, sometimes losing - and eventually signed a peace treaty with them under which Zakynthos was obliged to pay an annual tax to the Port. When the tax was left unpaid, the Turks sent their fleet to sack the island. The intervention of the Venetians ensured a delay in the Turkish landing, chiefly so as to give the Frankish inhabitants of the island the change to leave. The pillage finally took place in September 1479, and henceforth a Turkish garrison was quartered on Zakynthos. The Venetians, who at this time were busily expanding their possessions and influence in the Mediterranean, had for some time been aware of the value and significance of Zakynthos. In 1485 they persuaded the Port to cede them the island.

Venetian Rule (1484 - 1797)

The agreement of 1484 brought fundamental changes to Zakynthos and ushered in a new epoch for its people. Until then, the island's fate had been part of that of the rest of Greece. Venice had issued announcements in 1485 and 1492 in all its territories, inviting whoever wished to come to Zakynthos and make a new home. The Venetian nobles who held the reigns of government in Zakynthos generously shared out the farms and houses amongst the newcomers. A new period of activity began, which quickly resulted in high population growth.

An important feature of this demographic development was that the Zakynthian element was by no means wiped out. In the contrary, it not only recovered to a remarkable degree, but its influence was such that it assimilated the newcomers and permeated them with the characteristics of its own local traditions. Part of the reason for the growing prosperity of the island was, of course, that Venetian rile created conditions of peaceful stability such as had not been known for centuries.

One result of this was that the typical medieval settlement of Zakynthos which had been huddling close to the defensive strength of the castle, began to expand outside the walls and in time became a major town on the seaward slopes, with well planned streets, open squares, and imposing buildings. Known under the name of Aegialos, this fine new town came to be dubbed by the people of the time the "Florence of Greece". The islanders also began to establish settlements elsewhere on the island. The growth of the town, the promulgation of new laws, and the resurgence of commercial activities laid the foundation for the proper social organisation of the island. The usual aristocratic-oligarchic constitution was established by the Venetians and the population was divided into three classes:

- The nobles (Nobili), whose names were recorded in the "Golden Book" (Libro d'Oro).
- The bourgeoisie (Civili), who formed the middle class and enjoyed political rights.
- The ordinary people (Popolari), that is, the workers, farmers and sailors. They had no political rights and were effectively serfs.

It was indeed the insatiable and inhumane repaciousness of the nobility which in time led to serious social opposition and friction. By the beginning of the seventeenth century, this unrest dad become so acute that it led to the first social revolution in Modern Greek history. The 1628-1632 revolt of the people was drowned in its own blood by the Venetian Governor of the time.

Meantime, Zakynthos had contributed 7 galleys to the battle of Nafpactos on 7-10-1571. This epoch-making naval engagement decided the fate of Europe and buried forever the sultan's dreams of conquering the entire Mediterranean and the European continent in general. Venetian and Spanish vessels took part in it, as well as the Pope's ships. The Christian fleet also included some Greek vessels.

It is true, of course, that Venice was losing its overseas possessions. The people of Zakynthos watched this visible decline of its rulers and waited for the opportunity to cast off their yoke. With the spread of 18th century French liberal ideas and in the wake of the French Revolution, the people of Europe threw off the lethargy of subordination and organised themselves. Zakynthos received the new French ideas with enthusiasm. By the time Napoleon was winning his battles, political groups were being formed on the island, the most important among them the "Club of the Jacobins". The fundamental goals of the Zakynthos Jacobins were their complete political equality with the nobility. The ruling class on the island not unnaturally reacted negatively to this liberal movement. They had no compunction in stamping out the rebellion on the island. Only few voices turned down their agreement to kill the Jacobins.

French republic &
Russo-Turkish Domination

Despite the bloodthirsty stand of the ruling nobility on Zakynthos, the glorious republic of San Marco had run its course, The last Venetian Governor surrendered the town and the island to the French on 4 July 1797.

The local people celebrated the end of the oppression by pouring into the streets and squares joyously singing and dancing. Their euphoric celebration reached its climax on 30 July, when they publicly burnt the Golden Book in the triangular square of Aghios Mark, together with the coats-of-armed of the nobility, hated symbols of local oppression, and planted a "Tree of Freedom".

The French Consul, Charles de Guy, temporarily undertook the administration of Zakynthos, end formed a municipal council which was barred to members of the nobility. This council immediately voted the abolition of all aristocratic titles, and divided the island into communities administered by local mayors.

Under the French, Zakynthos became the administrative headquarters of the Prefecture of the Aegean and the democratic government began the difficult task of reconstruction. An important feature of this period was the establishment of schools for children from all the social classes. The first French presence on the island lasted only 15 months.

Even though all over Europe the winds of democracy were blowing away the old order the monarchical powers were doing all they could to reverse the trend. The Russians and the Turks prepared to take Zakynthos. On 25 October 1798, after a siege by the Russo-Turkish fleet, and after some of the pro-Russian nobles had handed the keys of the town to the besiegers, the French garrison was forced to surrender. This was followed by much violence between the nobles and the people, deliberately incited by provocateurs. Meanwhile the aristocracy managed to recover many of its privileges.

The Ionian State

On 21 March 1800, Russia and Turkey signed a treaty in Constantinople, which founded the Eptanissos State of the Ionian isles.

This State, according to the terms of the treaty, was to be a self-government part of the Russian Empire, and would pay an annual tax to the Port of Constantinople. This treaty with provided the nobles of Zakynthos with a new opportunity but the people of Zakynthos did not agree, and they began to revolt. One of their democratic leaders, Antonios Martinegos, organised a movement, which declared the island independent of the Eptanissos confederation. Playing on the acquisitive tendency of the English, the hoisted the Union Jack on the Zakynthos fortress on 10 February 1801.

But the hopes of the Zakynthos democrats had been premature. Seven months and a number of strange agreements between the Great Power later, the Turks and, to the chagrin of the Zakynthians, the English, returned the island to the Ionian State. The nobles for their part continued their machinations, which resulted in several new constitutions (1807), each more contradictory than the last, and eventually in another two years of rule by France, this time under the Emperor Napoleon.

Lithographs from the book by J. Cartwright,
"Views on the Ionian Islands".

The English Rule (1809 - 1864)

Eight years after the Zakynthos' democrats unsuccessful bid not to bring in the English, three frigates with 3,000 soldiers sailed into Zakynthos on 19 September 1809, took the fortress and hoisted the English flag. To begin with the English carried out a series on beneficial measures for the daily life and administration of the island, especially with then had been badly neglected, particularly among the lower classes. Another important event of that time was the foundation of a public printing-house in Zakynthos, which among other publications, brought out the "Newspaper of the Free Islands".

In 1814, England, Russia, Austria, and Prussia agreed that the island of the Ionian should become independent and form the United State of the Ionian isles. The English made sure of retaining for themselves exclusively the "protection" of the islands. A new constitution of 1817 laid the groundwork for tyrannical behaviour by the English, and the people began to rebel again. The first High Commissioner, Thomas Maitland, proved inflexible, violent and unjust, and the Eptanissos islands were once more the victims of their overlords' self-seeking. The people of Zakynthos now began a number of moves against the British Empire. On 23 February 1821 they despatched a petition to George IV, King of England, asking for the revision of the oppressive constitution. Although this particular petition had little effect, it was important for being the first of a series of official complaints and accusations by the people of Zakynthos against the English oppressors.

When the Philiki Etairia or the "Society of Friends" was formed to help free Greece from foreign rule, the people of Zakynthos were eager to co-operate and to give any help they could "Etairia" representatives Pangalos, and later Aristidis Papas came to the island and enrolled active members, founding the so-called Zakynthos Fighting Committee. The far-reaching activities of this committee earned it the name of the "Ministry of the exterior of revolutionary Greece".

The historical church of Aghios Georgios at Psiloma.

President of the committee was Dionyssios Romas and its members took their oath of allegiance in the little church of Aghios Georgios on the Psiloma hill above the town on the way to the castle, in the presence of the Epirote priest Anthimos Argiropoulos. When the Greek revolution was openly declared, the people of Zakynthos swelled with fresh hopes of liberation. Thousands of them went to the Peloponnese to fight by the side of their fellow Greeks, even though the English had strictly forbidden any assistance whatsoever to the insurgent.

The "Zakynthos Fighting Committee" achieved miracles. It provided asylum on the island for many refugees and sent money and men to support the cause.

The English occupation marked the zenith of prosperity for the island. Bridges built at this time are still standing today ands continue to serve the island's transportation network.

Part of the port's sea wall dates back to this period. The English also built many mansions on the outskirts of town on the old Venetian estates and undertook the restoration of, and additions to village churches, with their ever present and imposing bell towers. Of the many other houses built by the English on Zakynthos, not a trace remains today.

Union with Greece

British rule still held firm on Zakynthos and the other Ionian islands, however, not only during the revolution (1821), but even after the liberation and the establishment of the young Greek State. It was Britain's formal recognition of Free Greece, which heralded the start of new persistent struggles by the island peoples.

Their first step was succeeding in securing certain reforms of the constitution. The removal of censorship and the grant of a number of civil rights permitted the formation of three political parties on Zakynthos: the Radicals, the Reformers, and the Plutocrats.

The Radicals represented the broad and progressive layers of the people, and had as their main objective the banishment of the English "protectors" and the union of the Ionian islands with Greece.

The Reformers were more moderate, and merely advocated improve government under the English.

The Plutocrats were the tools of the English.

The proportion of representatives voted into the Ionian Parliament by the first free elections of 28 February 1850 was a direct reflection of popular sentiment: 30 Radicals, 6 Plutocrats, and 4 Reformers. On 2 December 1851 the Ionian parliament should vote on the union of the Eptanissos islands with Greece. Tough reprisals from the English followed this proposal, but the ethnic passions and determination of the people could not longer be held in check. Their struggles were now co-ordinated by the dynamic and fearless Member of Parliament and leader of the Radicals, Konstantinos Lombardos.

On 5 June 1863 a treaty was signed in London by England, France and Russia, under which England had to abandon her Status as protectors power and on 21 May 1864, the Greek flag was raised on the castle of Zakynthos and the people jubilantly celebrated their union with Greece. Now a part of free Greece, Zakynthos and the other Ionian islands shared the ensuing course of history with the rest of the country.

In the twentieth century, the new social, political and economic conditions that prevailed constituted to the definitive deterioration of the island. That which remained after 1900 was only the facade of the island's past grandeur. The earthquake of 1953 was a fateful event, which destroyed even the facade. A visitor today who wishes to discover traces of the past and to acquaint himself with Zakynthos' artistic heritage must not confine himself to the main town but travel widely throughout the island.

The monument of the "Philiki Eteria".

3

CULTURE & TRADITION

Customs & way of life - Music & Song
Popular theatre - People & professions
Arts & letters - Architecture

It is impossible to capture the beauty of Zakynthos in just a few lines – beauty that has been hymned by many poets and writers, both local and foreign. The island of Zakynthos has drawn the attention of many famous travellers and scholars from the beginning of the present century. It is the place where art and nature come together in a harmonious pairing.

To become acquainted with the character of Zakynthos we have to live its rhythms and observe its people and their way of life. With their weaknesses, the burden

of the historical conjunctures that they are called upon to overcome, the roots that they are obliged to defend, their minor differences and shared dreams, the people are always the best part of travel. Customs and tradition on the island, however, suffered a severe disruption after the tragic earthquake of 1953. We have to go back, to Zakynthos as it was before the earthquake, in order to understand how that tragic event abrutly severed the island's historic continuity, obliterating not only the town itself but also much of the evidence that would have been useful today in ascertaining to

what extent the old traditions had survived. Before entering the port of Zakynthos on its arrival, the mailboat would blow its horn 3 times. The long drawn out whistle brought all the towns people to the Strada Marina on the waterfront - those who were waiting for relatives to disembark as well as those without much to do who wanted just to find out who was coming aned who was leaving the island. Then the usually empty Strada Marina came to life and buzzed with activity. The arrival of the boat was always an opportunity for the local vendors, who invaded the boat with their decorated baskets offering for sale to the Cephalonians on board their special make of nougat, their powders, perfumes, icons and pamphlets on the life and miracles of Aghios Dionysios.

A gentle but persistent rivalry has always existed between the peoples of the two neighboring islands. The teasing and verbal playfullness between the Zakynthian "Nionios" and his counterpart from Cephalonia, "Gerassimos", has given rise to many tales and anecdotes which illustrate the sparking spirit of the islanders.

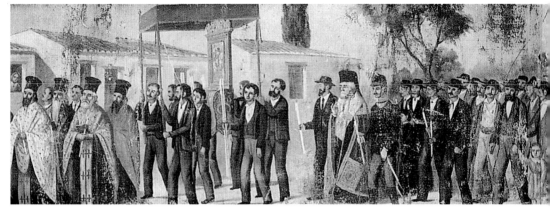

Customs and way of life

There are many local customs on Zakynthos, or Antetia, as they are known in the local dialect. The majority of them are connected with religion, which united the struggles of the locals against the conquerors.

During the period of Venetian occupation, much pressure was exerted on the Ionian islanders to convert to Roman Catholicism. Consequently, the people drew even closer to their own Orthodox faith, thereby strengthening both religious and nationalist tendencies.

One result was they made saints of three of the islanders themselves - Aghios Dionysios in Zakynthos, Aghios Gerassimos in Cephalonia and Aghios Spyridonas in Corfu - who were their own compatriots, sanctified during this period, and with whose relatives they fraternised in the marketplace. In this way they enhanced a feeling of mutual; trust and solidarity among all those whose fate it was to suffer the Venetian subjection. The islanders were therefore able to strengthen their morale and maintain their resistance to the occupiers. Their Orthodox faith thus became closely connected with political struggle, much as it had throughout most of Greece during the Ottoman occupation. And over the years, religious festivals became the forum for the islanders under Venetian rule.

Today, the occupiers are gone but the tradition of **religious festivals** were once dedicated on Zakynthos each year, is owe celebrated twice-yearly, on 24 August and 17 December, both with joyful celebrations accompanied by singing, dancing and fireworks displays.
On the Saint's Day, everyone celebrates and the islanders greet each other with the phrase "Chronia Polla" meaning " May you live for many years".

One of the most beautiful festivals to experience on Zakynthos is the **Easter** celebration. Easter gets under way on Holy Tuesday when the choir of the cathedral of Aghios Dionysios chants the traditional "Kasianis" palm. What makes this rite so special in Zakynthos is that the first Good Friday procession, beginning exactly at 2 p.m. (the hour, according to the bible, when the ordeal of Christ's crucifixions began) follows the figure of Christ on the cross.

For centuries now, this procession behind the cross has followed precisely the same route through Zakynthos town, beginning at the Church of Aghios Nicholas of Molos, cutting across Aghios Mark's Square on the main street and processing to the church of Aghii Saranta before heading back through Solomos Square to end at Aghios Nicholas church once more.

Venetian influences can be seen in the way Carnival is celebrated on Zakynthos. Striking costumes and lively dances give the island a cosmopolitan air during this period.

Then, on Good Friday evening, the procession of the "epitafios" itself takes place, a ceremony, which still echoes the grandeur of Zakynthos past. Today, during the " Epitafios" procession, a brass band lays the moving hymn traditionally sung for this occasion - a wonderful piece of music which is also something of a legend. According to well-documented sources, this impressive composition has been played during the Easter celebrations on Zakynthos since 1700, or even earlier. On Saturday night at midnight, after mass, (the ritual of Jerusalem is followed), the melodious bells of the cathedral begin chumming. It is the joyful signal to begin rejoicing to commemorate the resurrection of Christ. The band stroll through the streets of the town playing traditional music and the entire island celebrates late into the night. On Easter Sunday afternoon families gather to feast sign and dance and to celebrate one of the island's most joyful feasts.

The Zakynthos "**carnival**" was a product of Venetian society. The carnival period, which ends on the Sunday before the beginning of the Lenten fast, was once a time of merrymaking and revelry for all the islanders and its customs developed in imitation of the splendid, popular festivals of Venice. During the period, dances, were held at clubs, at people's homes, at local "tavernas" and even outdoors, in squares and public places. Square dances, quadrilles, polkas, mazourkas and waltzes were all performed with equal enthusiasm, as was the " yiargito" the "gaitani" (from a Turkish word mean ribbon) and the "tsakisto" (in which the dancers crouch suddenly, then leap to their feet.

The climax of the carnival began on Sunday afternoon, when the people gathered together in Zakynthos town's main St Marks square to enjoy the last bight of revelry. There is the traditional "Funeral of the masks", a symbolic rite, and dancing continues until late in the evening in Solomos Square.

Music and songs

One characteristic of the Zakynthian soul, and an inseparable companion of every islander, is music and song. On the Zakynthos of classical-era Greece, the god of music, Apollo, was worshipped. Own indication of how much the ancient Zakynthians revered music can be seen in the fact that the island minted a coin in honour of the musician Phytagoras, whose bust appeared on one side, with a lyre on the other.

Under the rule of the Venetians, the people became skilful players of a number of wind instruments, which they incorporated onto their music for religious and military processions.

The **Zakynthian "cantada"**, a song for four voices in harmony, is still the most beloved of these. Another type of song, the **"arekia"**, reminds us of the Cretan influence on Zakynthian music. Despite what has been borrowed from Byzantine and Italian music, Zakynthos has clearly developed its own local Ionian island flavour, reflecting the island's cultural legacies. A music school was founded there for the first time in 1815 and the following year the first Philharmonic orchestra was formed. Even these formal organisations were a natural outgrowth of tradition, since the people of Zakynthos had early on begun to gather together in choirs and other types of musical ensembles, developing their own talents and appreciation for music. Today the Zakynthos Philharmonic orchestra and the large musical associations, as well as the famous Zakynthian choir, carry on that tradition. This musical growth has naturally produced gifted musicians recognised not only on Zakynthos and the Ionian islands but even wider afield. The **ecclesiastical music** of the Ionian islands was very popular with a wide public that embraced its harmony and its joyful tones.

Descendants of Apollo and Pythagoras, the Zakynthians never miss an opportunity to sing the local serenades.

Homme et Femme de l'Isle de Zante

Inextricably inked with music and song, and of perhaps even greater interest, are the **popular dances** of the island, the most famous of which is the Zakynthos "**Sirtos**". A lively, spirited dance in two-quarters time, the " sirtos" is performed in every village, where it is known by a variety of names. It is danced to the accompaniment of tradition instruments - violin, accordion, and guitar or "tamborloniakaro" and the words of the songs speak mainly about love and marriage. Cultural events on Zakynthos are attended by older people wearing the appropriate traditional costume.

The Zakynthians of yesterday dressed according to the neighbourhood in which they lived and thus according to their class. The nobility wore silk garments with jackets of thicker material, waistcoats, black hose, silk socks and soft shoes. The ruling class wore wigs and shaved their beards and moustaches.

The lively dances and beautiful traditional costumes of Zakynthos.

Their women wore silk dressed with long trains. They also wore hats with masks or black veils, coloured socking, shoes with buckles and gold bracelets.

The bourgeoisie wore silk hats with tassels, hooded coats, coloured, knee-length trousers with 2 back pockets silk socks and buckles shoes.

The common people were trousers of a shiny Turkish fabric, waistcoats and sashes, white socks and buckled shoes. Their caps were white and they were forbidden to shave their beards or moustaches.

Popular theatre

Another exceptional folklorist element of Zakynthos culture is the popular theatre. This local tradition took shape during the period of the Venetian domination and its origins are connected with the popular Italian theatre of the Middle Ages and Renaissance. In 1571, they staged their first performance - " They Persians" by Aeschylus - and there followed comedies and other plays. These plays, however, were only performed in the salons of the aristocrats, and in Italian. In the last year of the Venetian occupation a small theatre was built for performances for the people. From the mid-19th century on, the passion of the Zakynthians for opera prevailed over the theatrical life of the island. Aristocrats and ordinary people alike threw themselves into the enjoyment of "belcanto" with all their hearts.

Of particular significance in the island; theatrical tradition are the plays known as: "Omilies" - which literally means "speeches". They were a form of people's theatre, usually written by an anonymous author so that he could freely satirise social in justice and the personal weakness of those in authority. It is not know whether the "Omilies" were brought to Zakynthos By the Cretan refuges or Whether, even before the fall of Crete, this form of Cretan theatre had reached the island. During the Venetian performed by men only, who disguised themselves with masks so that they could not be recognised by the audience. The female roles were played by the more elegant men. Social injustice and the greed and avarice of the nobles always had an important place in the "Omilies", which were performed outdoors. The "Omilies" in the "Chora" were only performed as carnival time, when the group travelled from one neighbourhood to the other with the show and finally performed in Aghios Markos Square, where the festival traditionally took place. The play was acted out in the middle of the square, filled to overflowing. Once it was over, the festivities began. One of the characteristics of Zakynthos' popular theatre is the way in which the local

1. *Female costume.*
2. *Drawings by K. Porfyris showing an "Omilia".*
3. *Zakynthians are always searching for new means of expression.*

actors view their activity. They do not consider the playing on "Omilies" a professional occupation but rather a part of their lives, something done joyfully, with: "kefi" (which translates as high spirits), a creative way of establishment warm contact with their fellows. The "Omilies", which are still performed today in the villages of Zakynthos in the villages of Zakynthos, are not restricted to old-fashioned themes. They often deal with contemporary social the scenario is old, the script is modern. Thus there is continuity between old and new-between thaw past and the present. In addition to the "Omilies" there were also amateur theatrical groups who also amateur theatrical groups who organises performances of ancient and medieval works on the island. An annual theatre festival was established on Zakynthos in 1965 called the "Conference of Medieval Popular Theatre". It takes place each summer, with performances of the Zakynthos "Omilies", and other works of Zakynthian and Cretan theatre, and with the participation of popular theatrical groups from Greece and abroad.

3

People and professions

The people of Zakynthos are full of zest, happy and hospitable, and represent all that is good in Zakynthian culture. They move about the town and the villages, shouting their wares. They chat in the market and let their hair down at the festivals. They are simple, yet profoundly cultured people, possessed of cultural self-sufficiency. They enjoy the little, simple things of life and therefore always love it. They have learned to endure pain and sorrow and wait patiently for joy and happiness to respect their traditions and customs. As bearers of an advanced culture, they have made sure that it is reflected in every aspect of their daily life in their every expression and occupation.

Zakynthian handicrafts and the rural way of life are poles of attraction for all visitors.

On Venetians times raisin production flourished more than the cultivation of olive trees as the yield was more profitable. During the Peloponnesians had brought the technique of raisin production with them when they settled on Zakynthos. After the war the foreign markets for Greek raisins were lost. Today the economy depends on the cultivation of olive trees vibes and citrus fruit, which yield the island's main export products - olive, oil, wine, raisin and fruit. The type of farming peculiar to Zakynthos (olive, groves, citrus orchards and vineyards) promoted the development of an unusual type of architectural construction - the "vergakia". Originally, the huts were used by those responsible for guarding and supervising the fields, providing a cool refuge from the hot sun and heavy work. Nowadays they are sometimes rented out, and some have even been built on beaches for those desiring a simple holiday hut right by the sea. Animal breeding and fishing have never developed significantly on Zakynthos.

Industry has never developed on Zakynthos, but has remained mainly at **cottage-industry** level. There are industries of this type that process farm produce, manufacture filler from dehydrated gypsum, which is quarried on the island, and traditional craft-industries making face-powder, candles and nougat.

For the last years **tourism** has sparked a significant development in the sector of summer apparel and **handicraft manufacturing**, carried on by small workshops and cottage industries. The villages of northern Zakynthos are the centres of this industry.

At the place, called Volimes, there is a profitable production of a rich assortment of woven goods, handmade lacework and embroideries, kilims and other tourist items for which Zakynthos is justifiably well known.

Examples of this tradition have been preserved in the private Vertzagio Folklore Museum at Pigadakia. Here, visitors can dream of times when the productive process was confined to methods and means very foreign to those of the present day.

1. Makeshift dwellings for the heat of summer (the so called "Vergakia").
2. An olive-press.
3. The reception room of a Zakynthian residence.
4. The traditional nook in which Zakynthian specialities are cooked.
5, 6. Wooden barrels for wine and vinegar and the machine for cleaning raisins.

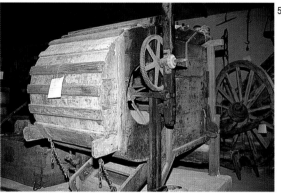

The development of tourism not only supplied an impulse to the economy but also gave the island a new form. Today the smiling island, with its peaceful life has become much frequented and sought after, especially in the summer when is host to scores of visitors, both Greeks and foreigners. The road has changed and been widened and there are no more quaintly cobbled streets.

Now the Strata Marina along the wharf is no longer the deserted road it once was, with the occasional idle passer-by. It now teems with life and motion Arrow of shops stretches from the church of Aghios Dionysios, offering every possible kind of souvenir.

Tourism on Zakynthos has always been a summer phenomenon, though the islanders should aim to extend the season to improve their tourist earnings. Zakynthos, moderate climate is very similar to that of the French Riviera, with abundant days of sunshine and mild winters without snowfall.

Zakynthos, however, is not only a natural paradise, ideal for holidays the whole year round, but is also a gourmet paradise. **Cooking** is a favourite pastime on the island; it has been handed down since ancient times and was later blended both with oriental elements and with the western tastes of the Venetian, French and British conquerors. Furthermore, the tourism that started to develop at the beginning of the 20th century has added dozens of gastronomic delights to the market.

One characteristic Zakynthian speciality is the famous skaltsotseta, an elaborate dish of veal and tomatoes, parsley, cheese and garlic. Dishes with seafood are also well-known, especially barbecued swordfish.

Finally, the famous mandoles and mandolato (nougat), and pasteli (sesame cake) are local items that should not escape the attention, and especially the taste, of visitors.

*The Strata Marina is always
full of life and movement.*

Art and literature

Few parts of Greece, particularly provincial Greece, can compare with Zakynthos with regard to the arts and letters, for there is virtually no sphere of intellectual or artistic life in Greece on which the work and personality of at lest one Zakynthian is not stamped.

The island of Zakynthos can be considered the backbone of Modern Greek Literature. The first Greek academy was founded on Zakynthos in the 16th century. In 1815, the Academy of the Free Western Islands was established, in 1812 the "Leschiotis" Academy and in 1829, the Medical Academy

The main spiritual guides for these academic enterprises were: **Antonios Martelaos** (1753-1819), the teacher of Foscolo, Kalvos and Solomos, a man of great perspicuity and wisdom who is said, on one occasion when Kolokotronis visited the island, to have addressed him with the words "I pay homage to free Greece".

Antonios Matesis (1724-1845), a gifted playwright: Georgios Tertsetis (1800-1875) and **K. Lombardos** a modern Greek historian. Then there was the italian -speaking **Ugo Foscolo**, born on Zakynthos in 1778, and the exceptionally distinguished poet **Andreas Kalvos** (1798-1863).

The most famous Zakynthian writer, who won both Greek and international recognition, was **Dionysios Solomos** (1798-1857) author of the poem "Hymn to Freedom". The first two 4-line stanzas of the poem were set to the music of composer Nicholaos Mantzaros, from Corfu, to become the Greek national anthem.

Form the recent past, one can single out **Grigoris Xenopoulos** (1867-1951) for his versatility in reducing both plays and prose of distinction, as well as for making a significant

Painting by Nik. Kantounis.

contribution to children's literature. He especially gained fame after the 1953 earthquake, when his works became the only exiting source of rich descriptions of Zakynthian life and traditions.

Zakynthos, at the crossroads of East and West, has felt the aftershocks of the powerful movements of history in every era. A sudden economic boom, based an agriculture and trade and on the formation of graft guilds in the 17th century permitted a flourishing of the arts on the island. And when the Ottoman Turks overran the island of Crete, many Crete artists immigrated to Zakynthos and played a significant role in shaping the art and technique of icon painting (hagiography) there (1669). In **post-Byzantine icon painting**, egg washes were used on wood. This technique is a blend of Byzantine and Renaissance methods and the tradition began on Zakynthos.

Painting in Zakynthos was also tied to the **Ionian School** of naturalistic art, heavily influenced by the Italian Renaissance.

It expressed the social and ideological characteristics of the new ascending force on the island - the bourgeoisie. With the 18th century came a real break with the Byzantine tradition which paved the way for the icon painters Panayiotis Doxaras, N. Kantounis and others who gave their art a more naturalistic dimension, far removed from the severe, expressionless figures of Byzantine church-painting. **Panyiotis Doxaras** was the first painter whose art diverged from traditional religious painting. In his work can be detected the roots of the Ionian School. **Nikolaos Koutouzis** studied in Venice and, after his return to Zakynthos, his work bore the imprint of all that he had learned there, most characteristically the use of chiaroscuro; in some of his works, this led to the creation of a tradition on Zakynthos.

1. The cenotaph of O. Phoskolos, with the sculpture "Lamenting Spirit".

2. Statue of Dionysios Solomos in the square named after the poet.

N. Kantounis is the most important painter of the Ionian islands. He studied under Nikolaos Koutouzis and very successfully imitated some of the great artists of the West, as well as his teacher.

Other painters of the 19th century including **A.** and **G. Gryparis**, **K. Giatras**, carried on the tradition, expressing through their icon portraits an atmosphere reminiscent of the Zakynthos "cantades" and "opera", another well-loved musical form on the island. Their portraits, idealisations which reflected the culture of the Renaissance, nevertheless never veered too far from realistic human from and dimension.

Apart from sculptures from antiquity, of which very few have survived on Zakynthos, there are a great many important pieces of carved wood and worked silver. The most important woodcarver on the island was **Georgios Bafas**. There are today three magnificent pieces by him in the church of Aghios Dionysios: an icon of the saint, measuring 1,50 m by 1,20 m, a funereal urn, and a reliquary for his hand, decorated with a series of miniatures of rare artistic value.

The works of other Zakynthian woodcarvers that decorate churches, homes and even furniture is just as significant. This artistic tradition also had its origin in ancient times. Among the best known artists of this genre. The Zakynthos artist **Stephanos Xenopoulos** (the brother of the writer Grigorios) gained international fame and recognition mainly for his work in mosaics. A cartoonist and caricaturist at the start of career, Xenopoulos later studied art in France and dedicated himself to mosaicking. Many significant works of his can be found in museums and churches throughout Greece and in a number of other countries as well.

The sarcophagus of Aghios Dionysios, by Georgios Baphas.

Architecture

Architecture is another element in the culture of Zakynthos, which is now different from that of the period before the earthquake with regard more specifically to residential architecture there. There were three types of houses in Zakynthos town: The large mansions (of the ruling nobility), the houses of the bourgeoisie and those of the lower classes.

The mansions were mainly built around the edge of town and in the suburb or "repara", north of the municipal theatre (now the library) and on the seashore, The mansions usually had three floors with severe imposing facades of porous stone. On the first floor were the reception areas and on the second floor the bedrooms, There is insufficient evidence to allow detailed descriptions of the middle class and common houses.

They probably had two or three floors with wooden staircase leading up to the main living quarters. The exterior of these houses was influenced by that of the mansions, except for the first floor, which was built with a characteristic enclosed, wooden balcony called a "bodzo" protruding over the street.

Today, all of this has changed. Post-earthquake Zakynthos has none of the beauty of the original town; despite the efforts made to rebuild it as faithfully as possible according to the original.

There are no more old-style houses with their tiled roofs darkened with age. Instead, there are tall, freshly whitewashed buildings with modern balconies, large windows and spacious verandas which have little in common with the old grand - pre-1953 houses. Only the town's newly-built museums still retains some elements of the old Zakynthos, contained in a number of exhibits which illustrate the grandeur of the religious, artistic and social culture of the Ionian islands.

Many of these exhibits were made possible only through the efforts of a man whom foreigners have dubbed "The Knight of the Ruins" the pharmacist and scholar, and descendant of a noble family, Nikos Varvanis. It is amazing what this exceptional Zakynthian achieved. While the earthquake was destroying the town and fire was engulfing everything, Varvianis, helped by a handful of Zakynthians, was scrabbling through the ruins saving whatever he could of the remains of the old Zakynthos civilisation. These he carefully collected and stored in an undisturbed corner of his estate. "Hermitage", where they remained for a long time without anyone being aware of it. One can still admire many of the traditional elements, which help explain the history and special character of Zakynthos.

It is in the **churches** of Zakynthos that one can see the splendid interrelation of the work of the island's gifted painters, sculptors, woodcarvers and gold and silversmiths. The churches different and are still different form the churches in the rest of Greece, although they are similar to those on the other Ionian islands. There is not one of the Byzantine style. Due to the influence of the West, the main building of these churches is long and low with the number of vaults varying according to how large the church is. There are also differences in the interior decoration, which is mostly influenced by Western technique. There is a very secular flavour in the interiors. The women' quarters are such that one balcony of a theatre or opera house. Thus one does not have the feeling of being in a place of worship.

Today the greatest pride of the Zakynthos churches is their decorative woodcarvings and silver work. Even the churches that were built after the earthquake still have their carved altar-screens. The main church of Volimes was even rebuilt around its remaining altar screen. In the town some of the finest churches are Aghia Triada, on the road to Krioneri, Aghios Lazaros on the other side of town and Our Lady of the Angels near the Hotel Xenia.

An essential but differentiating characteristic of every church is its bell tower. It stands as a kind of symbol, the pride and boast of its parishioners. The tunes that the bells ring out are easily recognise by the inhabitants. Of course, the musical sensibilities of the Zakynthians are well known.

The church of Aghios Ioannis at Lithakia.

4 THE TOWN

The town of Zakynthos – known as Chora, apart from its official name-is a new town, lying in a semi-circle between the foot of the Castle hill and the sea. It stands on exactly the same site, as did the town, which was wrecked by the earthquake and the fire of 1953. The new buildings have attempted to retain the style of those they replace –a mixture of Neo-classical and Venetian, with a strong dash of an entirely local atmosphere.

The efforts to conserve as much as possible of the old form of the town have involved not only its architectural aspect, but also its town planning fabric. It could be said that the layout of the town is roughly the same as it was before the earthquake. There is a long esplanade, the Strata Marina, behind which is the main street, once called the "Plateia Rouga" and now Known as Alexandrou Roma St. because of the hill which rears up behind it, there are few streets running parallel to the seafront, but those which are at right angles to it are of a particular interest. To the north and south, the town embraces the foot of the hill. Most

OF ZAKYNTHOS

of the building that is being done today takes place in the southern part of the town. Our visit to the town (Chora) forms the beginning of our tour, and is the starting point for our visit to the rest of the island.

In antiquity the settlement here stood up higher up on the flat top of Castle hill. It was on this hill that the ancient acropolis of Psophis was built and on which the Venetian City stood in later times. With the passage of time, the growing population and the changing living conditions caused the city to expand along the strip of ground between the foot of the hill and the sea. Because this strip was narrow, the town stretched out along the shore. Later still, the trade in the new harbour, and commercial activities of the islanders and the continuing growth of the population made necessary the filling in of the shore with earthworks for further expansion: the church of St Nicolas on the Mole (see the town plan) was once on an island, and a bridge linked it to the island. Solomos Square too stands on filled land.

▲ MACHERADO
ALYKES
VOLIMES

✝ Agios
Lazaros

33

AGIOU SPIRIDONOS

ISSAVET MARTINE

AGIOU LAZAROU

EPISKOPOU POULOU

DOMENEGINI

AGIOU GEORGIOU

YFANTOURGIOU

ETHNOMARTYRON

ARVANITAKI

PLATIA
AGIOU PAVLOU

ANASTASIOU TAVOULARI

KOUTOUZI

TERTSETI

Analipseos ✝

ALE

Airport
LAGANAS
KERI

◀ STAVROPODI

OMIRON

KALVOU

KATOHIS

GRITZANI

LISGARA

KANTUNI

GRIGORIOU XENOPOULOU

18

IOANNOU LOGOTHETON

MARTINEOU

MUNTSA

EVGENIOU

ROMA KANTIANOU

PLATIA
AGIOU LOUKA

GARZONI

GLADSTONOS

FILITA

TZOULATI

16

ANASTASIOU MERKATI

IOANNOU FILIOTI

15

AGIOU ELEFTHERIOU

19

FILI

FO

ERYTHROU STAVROU

TZANE

LASKAREOS

LISGARA

DAGIAPIERA

PLAKOTOU

MARTINEOU

DOXARADON

ARCHIEPISKOPOU KATRAMI

17

VALTERA

KATIFORI

LOMBARDOU (STRATA MA

Faneromeni ✝

DANIAS

VERNADAKI

IRINIS PALEOLOGINIS

TSAGAROPOULOU PROTOPAPA

GUSELI

KYPRION AGONISTON

AGIOU ANDREOU

EVGENIOU VOULGAREOS

AGIOU DIONYSSIOU

PLATIA
AGIOU DIONYSSIOU

🏛 Agios
Dionyssios

DANIAS

ARGASI
VASSILIKOS
▼

✝ Agios
Charalambos

◀ KALAMAKI

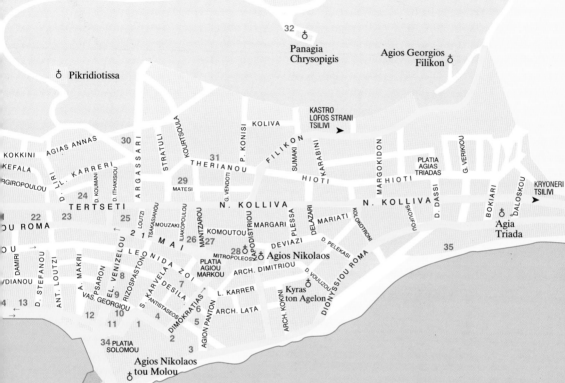

ZAKYNTHOS

LEGEND

1. Statue of Solomos
2. Library - Gallery
3. Statue of Vezal
4. Museum
5. Telecommunications (O.T.E.)
6. Ergobank
7. Labour Centre - Olympic Airways
8. Agricultural Bank
9. Commercial Bank
10. National Bank
11. Town Hall
12. Port Authority

13. Tax Office
14. Mortgage Bank
15. Ferry Ticket Office
16. Police
17. Electricity Company
18. Location of the house of Gr. Xenopoulos
19. Bus Terminal
20. Location of the house of Ugo Foskolos
21. Post Office
22. Alpha Credit Bank
23. Olympic Airways
24. Courts

25. Prefecture
26. Location of the house of Solomos
27. Ionian Bank
28. Museum of Solomos
29. Kalvou Square
30. Old Fountain
31. Secondary School
32. Bochali
33. Hospital
34. Statue of Foskolos
35. Organized Beach of the Greek Tourist Board
36. English Graveyard

We shall begin out tour of the town in **Solomou Square** (phot. 1, 3), which we reach from the central dock of the harbour. This is the town's largest square and is also its most recent, having been built - as we saw above - by landfill. Its lines of trees and pretty flowerbeds make it an attractive open space surrounded by aristocratic single - and two-storey buildings and with a state of Solomos, the national poet of Greece. In the centre, in the evening, this is where people consecrate for the "volta" the stroll which is a Greek provincial custom. New friendships are made and old ones renewed as the people of the town enjoy the cool of the evening.

In Solomou Square is the **church of Aghios Nicholas on the Mole** (phot. 5), the only Venetian building to have survived the fore and to have been restored - externally - to its original form. For many years it belonged to the guild of sailors. Next to the church is the Municipal Cultural Centre and the **Municipal Library** (phot. 2) housed in it, the Historical Archive, and the Phoskolos Cinema-theatre. Also in Solomou Square is the impressive building which houses the Museum of Byzantine Art.

Solomou Square and statues of Dionysios Solomos and Glory (phot. 4, 6).

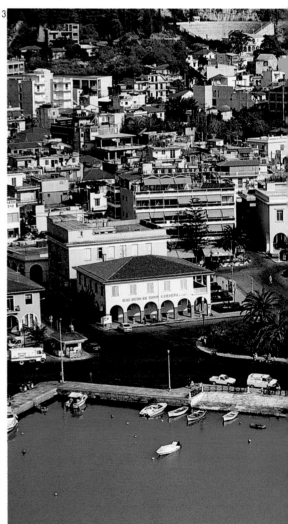

4

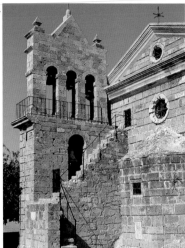

5

6

Museum of Byzantine Art

This is a well worth visiting; the route around the collection leads from the entrance to the right, up to the upper storey and along the whole building before descending once again. The Museum's rich collection of portable icons gives a very informative panorama of the local tradition in ecclesiastical painting, with works dating from Byzantine times to the 19th century and approximately one thousand post-Byzantine works in the Ionian and Zakynthian Styles. Among the painters whose works can be seen are Damaskinos, Tzanes, Kallergis, Doxaras, Koutouzis, and Tsonis. The earlier exhibits (some of them superb) are typical of the Byzantine style of icon-painting, while the works of Panayiotis Doxaras (1622-1700), who studied in Venice, are naturalistic and from the backbone of the Ionian school. This tradition was continued by Doxaras son Nicholas and Nikolaos Koutoyzis (1741-1813), whose works can be seen in the church of Aghios Dionysios as well as in the Museum.

This collection also houses the screens from the churches of the Pantokrator and Aghios Demetrius, together with the exterior of the little church of Aghios Andrea at Volimes. There are also Hellenistic and Byzantine sculptures and statues.

Vasileos Georgiou II St leads north from the Museum. On it stand the offices of the telephone company (OTE) and Olympic Airways. The street soon leads to **Aghios Markos Square**, known as *"Platyforos"* by the locals. This triangular square, with its cobbles, is a historic place: it is where the higher social classes of old Zakynthos gathered, and it is the town's oldest *"official"* square.

Here, in 1797, the *"popolari"* burned the hated *Libro d' Oro*, the *"golden book"* in which the names of the aristocracy were inscribed, after what the believed was liberation from Venice, by the French. In Aghiou Markou Square was the *"romianiko kazino"* or Liberal Club.

Today, the north east of Aghiou Markou Square, in Louka Karrer St, is the **Church of Our Lady of the Angels** (Strictly speaking, of the Presentations of Our Lady). This building was damaged by the earthquake but not totally flattened, and as a result it was possible to rebuilt it in the original Spanish *"plataresco"* style, with the fine friezes of Our Lady and the angels on the exteri-or and, inside, and admirable screen and wonderful icons by Panayiotis Doxaras and a number of painters in the Cretan style whose names have not come in 1687 and was the headquarters of the guilt of notaries.

As we enter the square, the Catholic Cathedral stands on our right. On the left is the Museum of Solomos and Eminent Zakynthians (it would be more accurately called the Solomos and Calvos Mausoleum).

The square of Aghios Markos at the night light.

Museum of Solomos

This interesting museum contains, on the ground floor, the imposing tombs of Dionysios Solomos (1798-1857) and the other great poet of Zakynthos, Andreas Calvos (1792-1869). In the entrance hall is a piece of tree in whose shade, on Strani hill, Solomos is reputed to have written his "Hymn to Liberty", which later became the Greek national Anthem, and his "The Free Besieged", composed in May 1823 to the distant sound of the Turkish cannon bombarding heroic Messolonghi. The tree stood on Strani hill until 1964, when old age overcame it. The rooms on the upper floor of the museum contain memorabilia of the great poet and of other eminent men of letters of Zakynthos, together with various collections, which have been donated to the Museum.

The street, which leads out of Aghiou Markou Square, is initially called 21 May St and then continues as Alexandrou Roma St. This is the Rouga Square, the main street of the town, as it always has been. For centuries the commercial centre of Chora has been here and the street owed its importance to its position on the heart of the town and to its arcades on the ground floor of the buildings and up the side-streets.

There was a dense market area at either and of the street Yiofiri, whose customers were chiefly the townspeople, and Aghios Pavlos, which traded with villagers entering and leaving the town. Today, the street is a lively, bustling place containing most of the town's principal shops.

From **Aghios Pavlos Square** we turn towards the sea front. On our right, two blocks back from the esplanade, is the triangular **Faneromenis Square**; the church of Our Lady "Faneromeni", which gave the square its name, was burned down in the fire of 1953.

Of course, the church was rebuilt together with its belfry, and today it looks just as it used to from the outside; inside, however, its artistic treasures have gone. A very few icons of the many important art-works it contained were saved and can be seen in the Museum of Byzantine Art.

Faneromenis Square differed from Aghios Markos Square in that it was the meeting place for the ordinary people of the town.

We continue in the direction of the esplanade, coming to the park and the sea-front avenue called the Strata Marina.

A large number of side-streets (kantounia) run from the **Strata Marina**, linking it with Rouga Square and the streets parallel with it, forming a dense network of streets in which visitors can wander at will, using as their reference point the sea, which can be seen from every little alley.

The Strata Marina is the town's second most important street; it starts in Solomou Square and runs as far as the church of Aghios Dionysios, patron saint of the island. In earlier times it was a commercial area. Today it is still Chora's busiest street, with crowds of people at almost all hours of the day and night: travellers disembarking from the ferries, visitors looking in the windows of the souvenir shops, local people continuing the evening stroll which began on Solomou Square, and people of all kinds eating and drinking in the attractive bars and restaurants.

On the Strata Marina are most of the travel agencies which organise trips to various parts of the island and boat rides right around it. The street also contains the ferry boat ticket agency and the bus station.

1. The Dionysios Solomos Museum.
2. The tombs of Solomos and Kalvos.
3. The Strata Marina by night.

Night view of the port.

Church of St Dionysios

The large church of Aghios Dionysios dominates the southern end of the Strata Marina. Aghios Dionysios is the patron saint of the islands and many of its boys bear this name. He lived n the late 16th and early 17th centuries, and is known principally for his monastic life on the isolated Strophades islands, to the south of Zakynthos.

Later, when he found himself in Athens on his way to the Holy Land, he was ordained Bishop of Aegina. However, a sick man and wishing to return to the monastic life, he resigned from office and retired to the Anafonitria Monastery in the North of the island.

His church - one of the three buildings not demolished by the earthquake - is a relatively new building, erected in 1948 to a design by Professor Orlandos. Externally, it s not particularly striking, with the exception of its size and its imposing bell-tower, a copy of that of St, Mark in Venice. This bell-tower has become something of a symbol of the island, since it is among the first features, which one discerns as one approaches on the ferry.

Inside, however, it has superb wall paintings with scenes from the life of the saint. The Church also contains paintings by Nikolaos Koutouzis and Doxaras.

The silver larnax in which the relic of the saint is an outstanding piece of work by Diamantis Bafas. The saint's memory is celebrated on 24 August, the date on which his remains were brought from the Strophades in 1716, for greater safety, and on 17 December, anniversary of his death in 1624. The celebration on both these occasions are most impressive, and the saint's relics are carried in procession round the town.

This brief walk around the town is, of course, only a first acquaintance. Although the town of Zakynthos is not old, it is an attractive place and one can spend many happy hours exploring its alleys.

We leave form Aghiou Markou Square. The road soon begins to climb and, after passing the newly built Municipal Amphitheatre, we leave the last houses behind. Soon after this a sharp turning on the left leads to the **Church of Aghios George ton Filikon** (Of the Society of Friends) (see History, page 26). The Society of Friends formed in the early years of the 19th century. It was a secret association of those dedicated to freeing Greece from Turkish rule. On the wall inside the church there is a list of the members sworn into the Society.

The castle hill, under which Zakynthos town stands, acts as a natural magnet for visitors. On hot summer evenings it is considerably cooler than the town, while at all times of the year it provides superb views. A stroll up the Bohali takes about 3.4 hr in each direction.

We continue up the hill. The turning right leads up to **Strani Hill**. It was here, under the trees, that the national poet Dionysios Solomos would walk, from his mansion which stood in the same area Indeed it is said that here he wrote "The Hymn to Liberty", which, set to music by Nikolaos Mantzaros, became the Greek nationalist anthem. The site of the Poet's mansion is a little further along the hill top; it was here listening to the cannon - fire from the siege of Messolonghi, where Byron met his end, that the wrote "The Free Besieged", one of the greatest and most inspiring modern Greek poems. This road continues down to Akrotiri through a pretty olive forest. This slope was where the houses of the rich were in bygone days. Returning to the junction, we turn left, following the signpost to Bohali. The road runs between trees and occasional houses with gardens and courtyards full of lowers and soon reaches **Bohali**, where it ends. Bohali's main beauty, apart from its charming houses and gardens, is its terrace overlooking the town and the south-eastern part of the island, with the mainland coast in the background. There are cafes and restaurants, most of which also have live traditional music in the evenings. The church of Our Lady "Chrysopigi" ("Of the Golden Spring"), which stand here and its visible from much of the town below, has a miraculous icon.

Naval Museum

The Naval Museum of the Ionian Islands, the first such Museum in these islands, was inaugurated on 16 June 1997 by the Navy. It is at Bochali, an enchanting site dominating the island near the Strani hill and the Kastro. The museum contains 140 original water-colours, to be found nowhere else in Greece, that represent the course of Greek naval history (from 1700 BC in ancient times to the Byzantine period, the Greek War of Independence, and the 20th century), and which are rare depictions of the ships of the Byzantine period.

Visitors can also see a collection of nautical items from well-known ships, such as compasses, anchors, helms and torpedoes, as well as models of ships, naval uniforms, books about ships and the sea, medals, photographs, etc.

Venetian Fortress

Above Bohali, reached by a cobbled path, which is a continuation of the road by which we arrived, is the Castle of Zakynthos. A Venetian structure of uncertain date, with fortifications reminiscent of similar castles all over Greece (and particularly of Rethymno in Crete), the fortress is now heavily overgrown with pines, but has even finer views, in all directions, than those which can be obtained from bellow. We enter through the outer gate, with its lions of Aghios Mark, and then pass through two inner gates before entering the site of what was once medieval Zakynthos. At one time there were four catholic and eight orthodox churches here, quite apart from the houses and other buildings, but the earthquake completed the damage that time and neglect had already wrought.

This Venetian fortress is said to have been the site of the fortificatio walls of the ancient acropolis (Psophida), which encircled the summit of the hill. The monuments discovered by excavations here are a total of 6 churches and five public buildings. All that survives of them are the parts that survived the devastating earthquakes that have struck the island. The church of the Sotir, or Pantokrator or Domo Sua Salvatore is a Byzantine church on the north-west side of the fortress that served as the Catholic cathedral.

The church of St Francis of the order of Minorites is a three-aisled basilica dating from the 14th century, the largest part of which was completed during the period of British rule. The church of Aghia Varvara is a small, aisleless chruch that stood near the Venetian prison, and the church of Aghios Ioannis Prodromos, which dates from the late 15th century, is dedicated to Aghios John the Baptist, at that time the patron saint of the island. Parts are preserved of the churches of the Panaghia Laurentena and Aghios Ioannis Prodromos, both of which date from the late 15th century.

Relics of a by-gone era in the Castle of Zakynthos.

TOUR OF THE ISLAND

To facilitate your tour of the island, we have selected three itineraries and suggest them to you in the hope that they will find you in the best possible mood to enjoy the result.

1. **South - east Zakynthos** is famed for its lovely beaches, some popular and others remote and inaccessible.

2. **North - west Zakynthos** is ideal for people who love nature and challenges.

3. **Central - west Zakynthos** offers tours of monasteries and peaceful villages.

During the summer period, you can also join an organised **tour around the island in a caique**. Whatever itinerary you decide on, the beauties of Zakynthos will reward you.

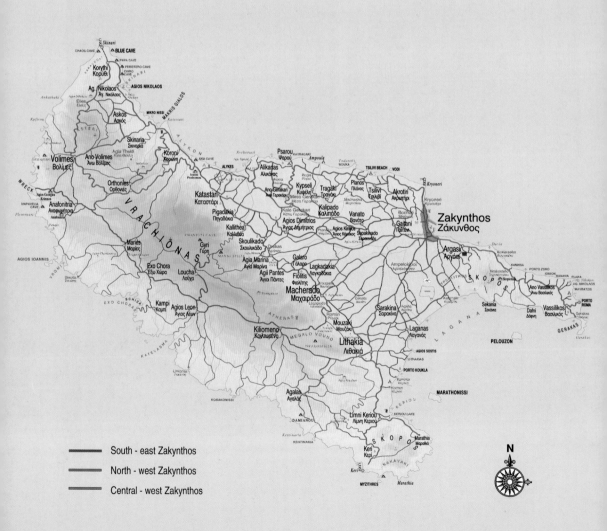

--- South - east Zakynthos

--- North - west Zakynthos

--- Central - west Zakynthos

Don't miss

1. CHURCHES

- *Aghios Georgios of Filiki, see p. 26*
- *Aghios Nikolaos of Molos, in Solomos Sq. see p. 52*
- *Aghios Dionnysios in the town, see p. 60*
- *Panaghia Chrysopigis in Bohali, see p. 61*
- *Aghios Charalambos, see p. 68*
- *Aghia-Ekaterini-tou-Sina, see p. 68*
- *Panaghia in Mouzaki, see p. 78*
- *Aghios Nikoalos in Mouzaki, see p. 78*
- *Saviour at Pantokratoras, see p. 78*
- *Faneromeni at Lithakia, see p. 78*
- *Panaghia of Keri in village of same name, see p. 83*
- *Aghios Nikolaos on Gerakari hill, see p. 87*
- *Aghii Theodori at Katastari, see p. 91*
- *Aghios Dimitrios at Ano Volimes, see p. 94*
- *Aghia Paraskevi at Meses Volimes, see p. 94*
- *Aghia Varvara at Pigadakia, see p. 100*
- *Chapel of Aghios Nikoalos (in the settlement of Draka, outside Skoulikado), see p. 101*
- *Aghia Marina in village of same name, see p. 101*
- *Aghia Mavra at Macherado, see p. 102*
- *Presentation at Macherado, see p. 102*
- *Aghios Nikolaos at Kiliomeno, see p. 106*
- *Saviour at Lagopodo, see p. 106*
- *Aghios Leontas in village of same name, see p. 107*
- *Maria Magdalene in Maries, see p. 109*

2. MONASTERIES

- *Panaghia Skopiotissa on Mt Skopos, see p. 68*
- *Panaghia Dermatousa at Tragaki, see p. 86*
- *Ioannis Prodromos (John the Precusor) on Mt Melissa, see p. 91*
- *Panaghia Spiliotissa at Orthonies, see p. 93*
- *Aghios Andreas of Kato Volimes, see p. 94*
- *Panaghia Elefttherotria at Macherado, see p. 102*
- *Yperagathou at Kiliomeno, see p. 106*
- *Anafonitria in village of same name, see p. 112*
- *Aghios Georgios of Krimni after Anafonitria, see p. 113*

3. SITES OF HISTORIC INTEREST

- *Vestiges of ancient temple of Artemis Opitais at Aghios Dimitris, see p. 61*
- *Old castle before Lagopodo, see p. 78*
- *Castle on Strani hill, see p. 100*

4. SITES OF SPECIAL NATURAL BEAUTY

- *Kmares in Marathia, see p. 80*
- *Mysithres at Keri, see p. 83*
- *Blue caves at eastern end of cape Schinari, see p. 96*
- *Gremos tis Fokias, southward of Schiza, see p. 108*
- *Navaghio beach on the Aghios Georgios, see p. 110*

5. SITES OF ECOLOGICAL INTEREST

- *In Lagana bay an Gerakas, there are special kiosks run by MEDASSET, (the Mediterranean Association to save the sea turtles) to provide informatin to friends of Caretta caretta, see p. 17*

6. MUSEUMS

- *Byzantine Museum in Solomos Sq. in the town of Zakynthos, see p. 54*
- *Museum of Solomos and famous people of Zakynthos in Aghios Markos Sq., see p. 56*
- *Maritime Museum in Bochali, see p. 62*
- *Folk Museum in the village of Pigadakia, see p. 100*

7. BEACHES

- *Argasi, see p. 68*
- *Aghios Nikolaos, see p. 68*
- *Porto Zoro, see p. 68*
- *Porto Roma, see p. 70*
- *Yerakas, see p. 70*
- *Ipsolithos, see p. 74*
- *Laganas, see p. 74*
- *Porto Koukla, see p. 79*
- *Keri Lake, see p. 80*
- *Tsilivi, which has been awarded th blue flag, of European distinction, see p. 86-87*
- *Psarou - Katregaki, see p. 87*
- *Alykes, see p. 90*
- *Alikana, see p. 90*
- *Makrys Gialos, see p. 97*

5 SOUTH-EAST

Argasi - Porto Zoro - Porto Roma -

After our tour of the charming capital of the island, we invite you to visit the picturesque little villages that add their own tone to the enchanting landscape. You would do well not to confine yourself to the organised tours that include the well-known tourist centres, but to choose one of the alternative routes that we recommend and explore the island, discovering its hidden beauty.

ZAKYNTHOS

Yerakas - Laganas - Lake Keri - Myzithres

This route takes in the peninsula in the south-east of the island and visits many of the most beautiful beaches on Zakynthos, some of them very popular and others remote, ideal for those who are trying to get away from it all. It calls at the most frequented beach on Zakynthos, at Langanas, and ends at cape Keri, the southernmost point of the island.

Argasi.

We begin on the coast road and cross over the bridge of the Aghios Charalambos ravine. Here a church dating from 1729, with some old icons and a gilded wood-carved iconostasis, has been proclaimed an archaeological monument. After the bend in the road we encounter the little church of Aghia Ekaterini-tou-Sina (St. Catherine of Sinai). On the other side of the bridge, we turn left and enter the district of Argasi; the road to the right ends at Lake Keri.

Argasi is a verdant valley, in which rises Mount Skopos, which is covered with orchards and greenery, and has red villas with vines growing over their courtyards and walls. The modern tourist villas nearby and the large beach make Argasi one of the most popular summer holiday resorts on the island. On the last Sunday before Lent, there are great festivities here with local dancing, feasting and drinking.

Short distances from Argasi are the ruins of a medieval tower. Beyond the village, the road turns inland and starts to ascend. A road on the right, after a quarry, leads to the top of Mount Skopos (485 m) – a walk of about 45 minutes, passing by the ruins of the **monastery of the Panaghia Skopiotissa**, dating from the 15th century. In olden times, when the people of Zakynthos were threatened by epidemics, or by pirate raids, they used to take the icon of the Virgin to Chora, to protect them. All that survives today is the church, which can be seen from all over Zakynthos. There is a breathtaking view from the top of the mountain, and the Venetians quite properly called it Belvedere ("fine view").

The public road continues, some distance from the sea, amidst lavish greenery, comprising mainly cypresses planted amongst other trees, a combination that is a characteristic feature of the landscape of the Ionian islands, and one of its most beautiful attractions.

We continue along the Argasi road, passing through Xerokastello, and come to the unmetalled road that leads to Porto Zoro (500 m). The steep road leads down to a beautiful little beach. It now runs through a fine pine forest. From here there are many side-roads leading to beaches.

Aghios Nikolaos is a little settlement with coffee-houses and hotels, and with a large sandy beach, 2 km away.

1. The monastery of the Panaghia Skopiotissa.
2. The village of Aghios Nikolaos.
3. The beach of Porto Zoro.

At the end of the main road, some 15 km from the town of Zakynthos we come to a fork in the road. The road to the left leads to **Porto Roma** (1.3 km), one of the most popular and beautiful beaches on the island, surrounded by green vegetation that comes right down to the crystal-clear sea.

To the right, the road leads to Yerakas (1.3 km). It is a superb beach set in spectacular surroundings that is protected on the south by a rocky peninsula. **Yerakas** is also a nesting ground for the caretta caretta sea turtle, and that is the reason for which there are restrictions on the development of the area and the activities of holidaymakers.

On the beaches of Zakynthos, the green of the land is reflected in the blue of the sea, creating astonishing colour combinations (Porto Roma, phot. 2, Yerakas phot. 1, 3).

Although we leave theoretically entered the village of **Vasilikos** visitors expecting to see a concentrated settlement will be disappointed. The houses of Vasilikos are spread over a wide area, amidst greenery and abundant water, farms and orchards. All these, together with the beautiful beaches, make Vasilikos another impressive sight. A rough track climbs sharply up on the right (signposted Dafni). Fork rights on toe the cement track as it ascends and then, at the top of the hill continues straight for **Dafni** (3,2 km from the main road). This is a beautiful unspoiled beach (Minimal facilities), facing the islet of Pelouzo in Laganas Bay. However, restrictions apply to the beach because the turtles use it for nesting. From the top of the hill a road to the right leads to Sekania beach.

From the top of the hill a road to Sekania beach.

Laganas.

After cape Yerakas we return to the town of Zakynthos and continue along the right fork in the road, which now leads us to Lake Keri. We start out on the coast road in the town and head south. We pass the road to Argasi and turn right, coming to Kalamaki and Ypsolithos, the latter with a superb sandy beach and limpid sea. Argillaceous rocks glisten in the most unlikely position in the crystal-clear water. Shortly after Ipsolithos to the south, along the waterside (reached only by path) is the huge rock known as the Vrontolithos. At its foot is a large cave, open towards the sea.

After 1.8 km begins the **area** known as **Abelokipon**. The Bay of Laganas with its two islands, one of the island's most beautiful - and also most highly developed - spots opens up before us. The sandy beach of Laganas (5 km from town) in longest in Greece. Wide ranges of sea sports are available. **Laganas** is a new village, which sprang up purely to serve the growing tourist trade on the fine beach. This is undoubtedly the part of the island to come to for restful holidays. The beach of Laganas is 9 km long, making it the largest on the island and one of the largest in Greece. The beach has much to offer sports-lovers, and visitors will certainly not be bored. In any case, the village in this area was created specifically to cater for tourist needs, which are steadily increasing.

Laganas: a tourist resort offering a wide variety of options (phot. 1-5).
The beach of Kalamaki to the right (phot. 6).

Off the coast at Laganas lies the islet of **Aghios Sostis**. *Once the islet was joined to the island itself, and there was a chapel to St Sostis on it. In the earthquake of 1633, the tip of the promontory split off and the islet was created. Here there is a picturesque little harbour with fishing boats and caiques. The islands, which lie in the bay, are called* **Pelouzo** *and* **Marathonisi**, *the later being heavily wooded. Olives, carobs, fig trees and bushes lie behind a beach of yellowish sand running down to emerald water. The road continues across the plain.*

Picturesque tones at Laganas (phot. 1),
Aghios Sostis (phot. 2) and Marathonisi (phot. 3, 4).

The main road, still running at some distance from the sea, enters the Mouzaki area. On the left can be seen the impressive bulk of **Sarakina**. Here very few Venetian country mansions have survived from the earthquake, though severely damaged by subsequent abandonment. The name of the house comes from the fact at one time the area was a hideout for Saraken pirates.

Mouzaki is a large villager famous for the quality of the water in its well. The history of the village dates back to 1521, and it has two interesting old churches: that of Our Lady bears the date 1741 on its carved wooden screen and also has a wooden ceiling, while St Nicholas, the village "cathedral" was built in 1815. Another large village, **Pantokratoras**, stands next to - and indeed almost part of Mouzaki High on the hillside above the villages is the old church of the Saviour; it seems to hang above the houses. The climb up to the church is worth the effort for the view, and also to see the treasures inside. On the side, the green plain stretches across to Chora with its castle, while on the other we can see Mt Scopos ant the blue fringe of sea at Laganas.

The church itself is a plain little basilica; the Byzantine double eagles carved into the floor, the screen is wooden, and there are old icons and the remains of paintings on the walls. According to local legend, the church was built by the Empress Pulcheria. Behind the church is an overgrown graveyard, and a little higher up the hill is a pretty well with carved masonry.

Following south direction we see the area of Lithakia. **Lithakia** is a village with old mansions. This has always been among the more prosperous villages of the area, thanks to its fertile fields in the Laganas area. Many of its inhabitants are also fisherman.

Just outside this village are the scattered remains of Paleokastro, one of the few archaeological sites on the island. Here, visitors can visit the old Venetian tower, part of which is still preserved.

1

From Lithakia, a diversion to the right of about 5 km leads to **Agalas**, a semi-mountainous village built amidst pine-forest overlooking the west coast. To the south-east of Agalas is the two-level cave of Damianos, with its stalactites and stalagmites. Four kilometres from Lithakia is a deep gorge called Avyssos, which has a spring whose water is reputedly good for the digestion. A clay path leads to a cliff-top from which the gorge can be seen twisting down as far as the sea. After Lithakia, a turning left drives us to the **Porto Koukla**, a narrow but attractive pebbly beach.

The road continues along the flanks of Mt Skopos or Megalo Vouno (meaning "big mountain", 423 m).

1. The archontiko ("mansion") at Sarakina recalls the grandeur of Zakynthos before the earthquake.
2. The church of Aghia Phaneromeni at Lithakia.
3. The cave of Damianos at Agalas.
4. The beach at Porto Koukla.

Sixteen kilometres away from town, a turning left drives us to **Limni Keriou** (1.1 km). This pretty hamlet lies at the head of the last cove before the rocky Cape Marathia facing Marathonisi. In ancient times, and until very recently, it was known for natural pitch wells, which were used for caulking ships and which gave it its venetian name of Porto Naphta. Attempts were made before the war to prospect here for oil, but despite the initital assumptions, they did not prove commercially viable and the workings have been abandoned. The wells by the beach have now been dried out but that described by the ancient author Herodotus may still be seen on the way down to the beach. At first sight, it looks like a pond of clean drinking water. But at the bottom a more careful look will reveal the black pitch lying among the green weeds.

Limni Keriou has a pleasant beach and cafes, and boat trips are available in approx. 1,15' hours to the caves, rocks, cliffs and little bays, which lie all around Cape Marathias.

After the turning for Limni Keriou the road climbs towards the neck of the cape. One kilometer away, a turning left drives to Marathias.

Marathias is an excellent pebble beach with deep, clear water. It has a fine view of Marathonisi. On Cape Marathias are two famous **Kamares** or arches, two huge rocks tower out of the crystal-clear sea to form a cove with a strip of tropically white sand at the end of it.

From the settlement at Lake Keri there is easy access to Marahtia (phot. 4), the famous spring of Herodotus (phot. 2) and nice area leading to the Cape of Marathonisi (phot. 3).

Keri (20 km) is a pretty village, built on the north-facing slopes of cape Marathias. There is an interesting church in the village, to **Our Lady of Keri**. According to the traditions, Our Lady hid the whole island of Zakynthos in a mist to stop it from being spotted by marauding pirates. The church is finely decorated. A track (very narrow in Keri itself and poor beyond) leads in 1,5 km to the lighthouse on the cape.

From here there are spectacular views of the rocky west coast of Zakynthos and the two white and huge rocks "**Myzithres**" which are dominating the scenery.

1, 3. Keri and the Myzithres.
2. The church of the Panaghia at Keri.

6 NORTH-WEST

Kryoneri - Akrotiri - Yerakari - Alikanas -

This route covers the north-east part of the island, along the coast, which has a large number of beautiful beaches. Several of these can be reached only from the sea. In this part of the island visitors will be entranced by the little villages and landscapes of outstanding natural beauty. Here the tranquil sea is abruptly interrupted by sheer rocks and geological formations of unique beauty,

ZAKYNTHOS

Alykes - Katastari - Volimes - Galazies Spilies

while the beaches offer their invitation to those who want to get away from it all and enjoy the wonderful Zakythian landscape. The north part of the island is wild and singularly beautiful, and is recommended for nature-lovers and those who prefer to discover a place by their own instinct and feelings. For these, the north part of Zakynthos is much more than a discovery – it is a revelation.

The Skourtis river.

From the coast road we head northwards and enter the suburb of **Kryoneri**, where the NTOG beach is (all facilities, entrance charge). The name Kryoneri ("cold water") comes from which passing ships used to take on water. The road continues almost due west near sea. This is the area which the Greek author Grigoris Xenopoulos (1867-1951), who was descended from a Zakynthian family, describes in his famous novel "The Red Rock".

Akrotiri, 2.6 km away from the town of Zakynthos, is a cool and healthy place among olive trees that is considered one of the closest rural areas to the town. In the pre-earthquake era, the country mansions of the rich were here. We can still see them today, half-hidden on the dense vegetation, but some are ruins and others have been rebuilt in a reminiscence of their former glory.

From here there is an excellent view of the sunset. The rock offshore is known a "**Vodi**" - the Ox - and there are a number of stories as to the reason why. The most common is that the shape of the trees, which stood on the rock, was reminiscent of the horns of an ox.

The road leaves the shore and descends through a series of hairpin bends. We leave Bohali on the left, we emerge from the woods and the **beach of Tsilivi** opens out beneath us. The blue sea stretches as far as Cape Yidakia (or Todaritis) which ends the curve of the bay.

Returning from the beach, we enter the **Planos** area, once a quiet village but now rapidly developing into a resort area and particularly known for its night-life. The road continues through olive trees and leads to some small and quiet beaches. We are now on the main road, with the villages of Marineika, Tragaki and Kypseli on the left, set amidst green hills and dense olive-groves. Tragaki is famous both for its natural beauty and for the monastery of the Panaghia Dermatousa.

At Kypseli, the old decoration is still preserved inside the village church. If we take the side roads leading from the main road, we shall come to the beaches of **Bouka** and **Ampoula**, both of which have been awarded blue flags, and to the equally fine beaches of **Psarou** and **Katregaki**.

Remaining to the basic road and 14 km away from the town of Zakynthos, we are already in the middle of the most attractive landscape of rolling hills, which bound the plain of Zakynthos to the north-east. At the right time of year, this is a fine place for walkers; the olive groves provide plenty of shade, there are old mule-tracks from village to village, and the scenery is very beautiful.

After 3 km the road descends round a series of bends with the striking bell-tower of the church of **Aghios Nikolaos** on top of Ano Yerakario hill always in front of us. Still following the main road, we pass Mesa Yerakari and Kato Yerakari and head towards Alykes.

1. *Kryoneri in the north part of the island.*
2. *The church of Aghios Nikolaos at Ano Yerakari.*
3. *Tsilivi beach.*

Alykes.

As we approach Alykes, there is a turning right for **Alikana**. 2 km the beach at the southern end of Alykes bay. Mycenean pottery has been found here, and the area is one of the possible sites for the ancient city of Arkadia.

Alykes, 24,5 km away from the town of Zakynthos, is one of the popular centres in the island. Argasi and Laganas are the most highly developed parts of Zakynthos. A marina is currently under construction at the end of the beach nearest Zakynthos town. The village gets its name from the salt pans behind the beach, where the road climbs to the village Katastari.

Alykes: a popular beach recommended for water-sports enthusiasts.

Katastari, the largest village on the island and a friendly one. This village has a peculiarity which is characteristic of Zakynthos. We go first through one half of the village, which is followed by a length of empty, road, giving the impression that we have come to the end of Katastari, and suddenly find ourselves in the second half, built amphitheatrical along the roadside. To the left rise the slopes of the mountain, and to the right, below, stretches the lovely bay of Alykes.

The combination of the mountain and the emerald-green sea, the "lake of Alykes", with the light glancing off its surface, the breathtaking vista from the "balcony" of Chartata, and the refreshing breeze, all afford relaxation from the heat of the day and restore the spirits. They make you feel you can't leave the enchanting paradise of the island.

The church of the Sts Theodoroi here is worth seeing if only because all the ecclesiastical treasures from the surrounding area - from churches, that is, which were destroyed by the earthquake - have been concentrated in it. This is quite a common practice all over the island; one church has been rebuilt and all the icons from the others installed in it. We turn right and begin to climb towards the hilly spine of the island. The road runs initially through olives and cypress trees, which we gradually leave behind. Turning for the far end of Alykes beach the road continues to climb and, as we look back, there is a fine view over Alykes, with the plain far in the distance. We pass on the left a turning to the monastery of John the Baptist, which stands a short way above Hartata the uppermost part of Katastari, on the lower slopes of Mt. Melissa.

The view of Katastari from Alykes.

We turn left to the **monastery of John the Baptist**. We do not know when the monastery was first built, but it was renovated on 1617.

The monastery belonged to Panayiotis Patrikios. Like other pious fellow-villagers he became a monk and left his estate to the monastery. The church has an icon of the beheading of Aghios John, which is a superb example of the work of the icon-painter Th. Poulakis. There is also an icon of the Virgin "the Joy of All" by G. Baphas, and a noteworthy wood-carved icon-stand.

The monastery church is a simple basilica flanked by the two-storey guesthouse building, which has a covered wooden balcony reached by a stone outside staircase. The main entrance is vaulted, with a relief of the Byzantine double-headed eagle; above is the belfry, with four bells, Inside the church as a good screen, old icons, and the double-headed eagle on the marble floor.

John the Baptist was the island's patron saint in the old days, before being succeeded by Aghios Dionysios. The monastery was a calling point for many villagers who lived in the mountainous parts of the island. In those days the town was a long way off, and the monastery offered food and rest to wayfarers and their pack animals.

Our road turns west and leaves the coast. We run through a kind of gorge into the centre of the northern part of Zakynthos.

Soon we meet the crossroad for **Orthonies** (1 km), a picturesque village with quite a number of old houses.

The monastery of Aghios John the Baptist.

From here, there is a good view of the bare spine of Mt Vrachionas, the highest point on the island (756m).

From Orthonies, the road continues (surfaced, 2 km) to the **Monastery of Our Lady "Spiliotissa"** ("of the Cave"), on the edge of a gorge. Founded in the mid-16th century. The same road heads towards the east coast, passing through low hills in the area of Koroni. Continuing along the main road, we come to a fork (26 km), at which the branch to the left leads to the Anaphonitria. We take the road to the right, which ascends through cultivated farms.

The verdant landscape at Orthonies confirms the outstanding beauty of Zakynthos and the Ionian islands in general.

We enter **Volimes** *(phot. 1, 4) 30 km.* The village actually consists of three settlements: Kato ("lower") and Mesa ("middle") Volimes, which are more or less united, and Ano ("upper") Volimes which stands slightly higher up the hill, which we shall return.

They are the centre of life in this part of the island. After the trip from Zakynthos it is a good place to stop for refreshments. Volimes is also famous for its cheese and honey and one can admire there the local handicrafts: Volimes is a major producer of the hand-made lace and rugs for which Zakynthos is justly famous. Ano Volimes is the island's most typical "mountain village". Here, the houses are built amphitreatically around the large church of Aghios Demetrius, which dominates in the centre. Meses Volimes has attractive alleyways leading to charming houses with miniature staircases, courtyards and pergolas. In the centre of the village is the large church of Aghia Paraskevi, whose tall bell-tower is an exact copy of that of Aghios Dionysios in Chora.

The church was built in 1633 and renovated in 1700. It has a carved and gilded screen, which is a true work of art, and the old ceiling is also in carved wood. The most interesting icons are the large silver works showing Aghia Paraskevi and Our Lady with Christ.

We leave Meses Volimes and pass through Kato Volimes before continuing to the ruined **monastery of Aghios Andreas** *(phot. 2)* ant the dense pinewood behind it. The view is wonderful from up here, with the two islets called **Diapori,** visible in the distance below the steep drop. We return to Volimes and take the main road, which in this case ends at the northernmost point of the island, cape **Schinari** *(phot. 3),* set in a picturesque bay. Just before Schinari, we come to Korithi.

Land, sky and sea in perfect harmony.

3

From Korithi we take the main road running parallel with the sea and after 2 km come to the **cove of Aghios Nikolaos**, with **Megalo Nisi** lying at its entrance. Caiques from here visit the Blue Caves, the voyage taking about one hour.

The **Blue Caves** are a series of geological formations in the cliffs beneath Cape Skinari. Apart from the natural arches produced by erosion, the caves are remarkable for the colour of the water in the deeper caverns: the refraction of the light makes everything in the water, the rocks and the boat in which we visit the caves, appear an unearthly shade of blue. A trip to the Caves is highly recommended, not least for the general beauty of the coastline, with its deep, clear sea. The colours are best (in summer) towards midday when the light is too strong. During the period of summer, the water obtains the most beautiful colours with the sunrise.

One can also visit the Caves by boat from Zakynthos (town) as a part of a trip round the island. From Aghios Nikolaos and during the season sof summer a ferry can drive you to

Pesado of Kefalonia. We continue through Aghios Nikolaos.

After 3 km, a turn to the left leads to the village of **Askos**. Proceeding for another 3 km. we come to **Skinaria**, where we join the road from Volimes. We turn left here towards the sea and after 3 km come to **Mikro Nisi**, where there is a Venetian villa built in the 14th century.

To the right of Mikro Nisi is **Makrys Yialos**, a golden beach with crystal-clear sea. To the south of Mikro Nisi, we skirt cape Kalamafka and come to a series of sulphur springs. The largest of them is the well-known cave of "Xyngia", where the waters are believed to have medicinal properties. The "Xyngia" cave is visited by caiques from Aghios Nikolaos.

The name of the area derives from the deposits of sulphur-bearing clay, which is called "xyngia".

Makrys Yialos (phot. 1), Mikro Nisi (phot. 2) and Aghios Nikolaos (phot. 3) are only a few of the beautiful beaches of Zakynthos.

7 CENTRAL &

Aghios Dimitrios - Skoulikado - Macherado -

This is the longest route and takes in north-west Zakynthos, more specifically the region around Mount Vrachion. There are very few beaches here and the coast is steep and rocky, so that this area is not suitable for swimming. On this route we shall discover a large number of churches and monasteries, with an impressive variety of architecture both in their exteriors and in the interior decoration.

WEST ZAKYNTHOS

Lagopodo - Aghios Leon - Kambi - Porto Vromi

You will often break your journey at some pretty tavern in a quiet village, where you can sample local Zakynthian specialities and the Zakynthian wine – recompense for the effort of travelling. After the first couple of glasses of wine, you'll be one of the locals, and will probably soon be singing the island songs as if Zakynthos were your second home.

The shipwreck.

We go straight on from Aghiou Markou Sq along 21 Maiou St and then follow the signs for Volimes. Three kilometres from the town we come to a crossroads: Gaitani to the right and Machairado (7 km) to the left, from which we shall return. Following the road towards Gaitani, we will then meet the village Vanato and the Kalipado.

In the village is a chapel belonging to the Voultsis family, one of the oldest clans on the island. The interior of the church is finely decorated, and many of the family ancestors are buried beneath the floor, as was for centuries the local custom. We keep on going straight, leaving on the right the village Sarakinado and then Aghios Kirikos, a beautiful village with picturesque places where you can have fun.

After Kalipado, a road on the left (10 km) brings us back to another point on the main road, and then to **Aghios Dimitrios**, which is of interest for its old churches and tall bell-towers.

At this village can be seen remains of the ancient temple of Artemis Opitais.

After Aghios Dimitrios, and about 1 km before Katastari, a road on the left leads to the village of **Pigadakia**. This is a mountain village dominated by the large church of Aghia Varvara, in which the treasures of the old church of the Panaghia Vlacherna are now housed, along with those from other little churches. At Pigadakia one can visit the private **Vertzayio Folklore Museum**, which has a display of objects representing another, traditional way of life.

Going now in the opposite direction (towards Macherado), we come to the pretty village of **Kallithea**, and immediately beyond it to **Skoulikado**, a settlement in the plain. This village has a tradition of music and of popular theatre, particulary the "Homilies". The plays are of Cretan origins, and include the "Arethousa", a version of the medieval love poem the "Erotokritos".

The variety of its church architecture is a feature of Zakynthos.

The church of Aghia Marina.

At the entrance to the village is the proud white-washed **chapel of Aghios Nikolaos**. It has a carved gilt screen, a wooden painted ceiling with the Pantokrator and the 4 apostles, and icons showing miracles worked by the saint. Next to the screen, on the floor, rests a large icon of St Nicholas. It is said that the face of the saint was discovered imprinted on to it four hundred years ago. The frame and the silver were added later to make the rock into an icon. As we climb up into the village, we see the 34 metre bell-tower of the church of Our Lady. In the centre of the village, in its large square, stands the School of Domestic Science in a new building.

Just 2 km from Skoulikado we come to the village of **Aghia Marina**. The older name of such village was Faghia. Here, the church of the same name is of outstanding architecture and some wonderful works of art. The church stands in the lower slopes of Mount Lalotis, on a site occupied by an earlier church erected in 1633.

The present church, which was built in 1855, has the shape of a cross externally, while on the inside it takes the form of a three-aisled basilica. It is also adorned by some notable works of art, such as a silver-sheathed icon of Aghia Mavra, a gilded wood-carved baroque iconostasis and a wood-carved bishop's throne.

The traditional stone bell-tower can also be seen in the forecourt of the church, and a guesthouse that functioned as a primary school prior to the earthquake of 1953.

The church occupies a fine site and is well worth visiting as well for as the panoramic view it offers and the wonderful architecture it presents.

Our next call is at **Aghii Pantes**, which used to be called Mikro Galaro.

After this we move on to Foliti, which owes its name to the family that first built it, and Langadakia.

The next stop on this route after Langadakia is **Macherado**, which lies about 30 km from the town of Zakynthos. Macherado is the second largest village in the plain, after Katastari. Its main attraction is the **church of Aghia Mavra**, which has very melodious bells that can be heard all over the island, so it is said. The church itself is a simple basilica, with no exterior ornamentation. On the inside, however, the decoration is surprisingly lavish and there are some fine works of art. The rich adornment of the interior of Aghia Mavra recalls the church-museum of the old Phaneromeni in the town, which was destroyed in 1953. It has a superb, gilded, wood-carved iconostasis, and it is worth pausing before the miracle-working icon of Saint Mavra, to see the ex votos hung upon it by the faithful.

According to another tradition, the saints it whom the church is dedicated (that is, Sts Timotheos and Maura) lived in Thebes, Egypt, where they were martyred in the 3rd century. The icon was brought to the island from Egypt by the Tzavarias family. The church celebrates its feast day on All saints (the first Sunday after Pentecost, usually in June).

With the exception of the feasts of Aghios Dionysios in Chora, this is the most impressive ecclesiastical event on the island. It is followed by feasting with traditional music and dance.

Machairado also has a **church of the Presentation of Our Lady**, restored by the Archaeological Service. It was built in the 14th century on a rise with a view over the plain to the castle and Mt Scopos. The Belfry is highly decorated, and although one of the island's tallest in not a tower-like structure such as that of St Maura. The northern side of the church has fine carvings in relief. Inside, however, it is something of a disappointment, as all the icons have been moved to Aghia Maura. All that is left is the carved marble screen and some marble column capitals, with a relief doubleheader eagle on the wall.

A little to the north of this church we come to the pretty village of Melinado. From here it is 10

km across the verdant plain of Zakynthos back to the town. The currants which were once the island's main and most famous crops are no longer grown extensively: they have given place to other products. There are crops all the year round, and even in the height of summer the plain is an oasis of green. The gateposts next to the road are all that has remained of the mansions flattened by the earthquake. The positions of the villages can be identified by their belfries, which can be seen protruding from the dense greenery.

After Macherado we come to the new, fortress-like nunnery of the Panaghia Eleftheriotria. There is a wonderful view from here over the Castle in the town and Skopos.

The church of Ypapandi (phot. 1)
and the church of Aghia Mavra (phot. 2) at Macherado.
The priveous page: The interier of Aghia Mavra.

2

Immediately beyond is the village of
Lagopodo, *where excellent wine is produced.*
There is also a fine church of the Saviour
here. The local wine reputed one of the best
in area.

Proceeding along the main road, we come
to **Kiliomeno**, *a village with traditional two-*
storey houses. Its earlier name of Aghios
Nikolaos was derived from the large church
of this name, which is well known for its
unique tower-like bell-tower. This imposing,
tall structure, divided into storeys with small,
round windows and a fine balcony, on which
are the bells.

After Kiliomeno, a side-road to the right
leads to the **Yperagathou Monastery***, which*
was built in the 17th century by two brothers
and dedicated to the Virgin.

The monastery now recalls little of its
brilliance of the period at which it was built.
There is just a large cistern at the entrance
to call to mind a variety of legends relating
to its origins.

3

Aghios Leon, 40 km from Zakynthos, is our next stop after Kiliomeno. This is a picturesque gleaming-white village, in which the church (photo 3) after which it is named was built in the 14th century and has a distinctive white bell-tower. In this village is a state-supported textile factory making carpets and superb fabrics. Beyond this village, a road to the left descends the barren hillside down to the sea (6 km).

Another road, on the right after 4 km, leads to Loucha (photo 4) and the village of Yiri. Loucha is curious in that you ascend the mountain, expecting to see it in front of you, but it suddenly appears in the distance in a small valley, nestling amidst cypress trees, perhaps out of "fear of pirates".

Yiri is 2 km further along, at a height of 550 m.

1. Place of pilgrimage in Kiliomeno constructed by the local craftsman from local materials.

2. Yperagathou Monastery.

After Aghios Leon, we continue once more along the basic route, and pause for a while at the little village of **Exo Chora**, which has a number of beautiful houses dating from before the earthquake. Just before we reach this village, we can turn left, to **Kambi** (2 km), a tiny village on the top of the rocks.

At the highest point of the village **Schiza** is an enormous concrete cross (phot. 2, 3), erected in memory of those killed here during the Civil War. Just beneath are some inviting cafes. On the way up to the cross are traces of a Mycenean burial ground. The views along the coast are superb, as is the sunset.

Slightly to the south of Schiza is the so-called Seal Cliff ("gremos-tis- fokias"). According to one version, it got its name from the Seals which come to have their pups in the large caves; another story connects the name to the seal-shaped rock at the entrance. The sight is superb: low pine trees run to the edge of the drop, ant then the rocks plunge vertically down to the blue waters of Seal Bay.

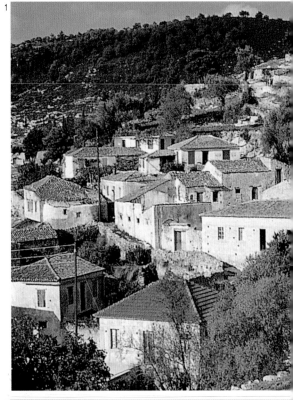

Maries (phot. 1), 33km away from the town of Zakynthos is a large, upland village swamped in greenery. Maries (33 km) a large, upland village swamped in greenery. It has a three-aisled church rare on the island-dedicated to Mary Magdalene, who reputedly stopped here (her footprint on a rock is shown) and taught Christianity on her way to Rome to protest over the conviction Of Christ.

The summit of Mt Vrachionas (called Vouni) can be reached from here in about one hour. The views across the whole of Zakynthos and over to Cephallonia are suburb. All the villages along the coast from here southwards have suburb sunsets- and cafes strategically placed to take the most of them. Maries runs down as far as **Stenitis** (phot. 4), a wonderful little cave with greenish-blue crystal clear water.

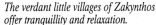

*The verdant little villages of Zakynthos
offer tranquillity and relaxation.*

4

Close to Steniti lies Porto Vromi (there is a road that can only drive you here from Maries and not directly from Stenitis). This is a spectacular trip along and down the precipitous cliffs of the west coast from Maries, with exceptional scenery. Care should be taken on the unsurfaced road. Down at **Porto Vromi**, a sheltered cove with swimming off the rocks and from a tiny beach Nawagio with coarse white sand, where the water is emerald in colour (no refreshments; take water), it is possible to take a boat trip along the coast for a swim and look at shipwreck.

From here, one can visit the island and two wonderful caves with funfare of colours. Apart from this route, that can only be run by boat, it is more frequent the northwestern direction from Maries to Anafonitria.

Beauty on four sides.

As we leave Maries, a little road on the left leads to the beautiful little mountain village of **Anaphonitria**.

If we return to the village, the other fork of the road brings us almost immediately to the **monastery of the Anaphonitria**, which attracts a large number of pilgrims. At the entrance to the monastery is a medieval tower with six machicolations, which is now used only as a bell-tower. A vaulted entrance leads into a garden, in the middle of which is the katholikon (monastery church) and the monastery buildings.

The monastery of the Anaphonitria awakens fairytale memories.

After the village of Anaphonitria we come to another fork in the road. The first road leads to Volimes, and the second to the **monastery of Aghios Georgios Krimnon**, which stands high above the sea in a lonely but enchanting landscape.

Inside this austere church is a white iconostasis with gold bordoures, old icons, and the characteristic double-headed eagle in the floor. Below the monastery is a path leading to the cave that was the home of the hermit Saint Yerasimos, the patron saint of Kephallonia.

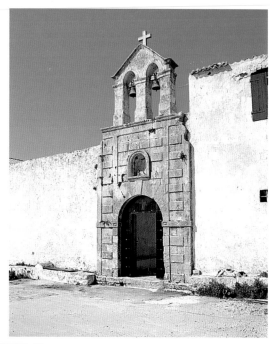

Isolated and imposing, the monastery of Aghios Georgios Krimnon.

Boat-tour of the island

Caiques starting daily at 9.00 from the port of Zakynthos make a tour of the island. Tickets should be booked at one of the special agencies to be found in various parts of Zakynthos. The route followed runs parallel with the north coast of the island.

The caiques start in the north-west and sail completely round the island, calling first at the **Blue Caves** (beyond Aghios Nikolaos and before Schinari). Here, visitors are taken to the Blue Caves in small boats, and can enjoy the crystal-clear blue sea from which the caves derive their name. The next stop, after cape Schinari, is the northernmost point of the island, the **Bay of the Shipwreck**. Here there are many sandy coves in the steep coast. Passengers may swim or sunbathe on a wonderful beach, before the shell of a shipwreck. The sea at this point is cold and very deep, and normally rough. The voyage then continues, to visit Marathonisi, beyond the pretty bay of Vromi, Karakonisi, the Keri Lighthouse, the caves of Keri, cape Marathia, and this entire region, with its steep coasts, which make it difficult to gain access to the island on this side.

Marathonisi lies opposite Lake Keri and Porto Koukla, where again there is a fine beach and clear water. You can also visit this point of the island by taking a small boat from Laganas, and there are also special glass-bottomed craft from which you can observe the turtle Caretta caretta. These turtles can also be observed on the island of **Pelouzo**, the next caique stop. The coast opposite Kalamaki, Sekania, Daphni and Yerakas is a protected area. It is forbidden to land or do anything here in the evenings, because this is where the turtles hatch.

From **Yerakas**, after a short stop in the verdant **Bay of Mavratzis** and **Porto Roma**, the caique returns to the port of Zakynthos in the late afternoon.

The nearby islets

The only islets of any note that belong to Zakynthos are the Sporades, which lie a full 25 nautical miles away from the main island, and which are discussed separately The largest two of these lie in the by now familiar bay of Laganas, which occupies the entire west coast of the island.

Vodi

This island lies off the north coast of Zakynthos, to the east of Tsilivi beach.

Aghios Nikolaos

This islet lies opposite the little harbour of the same name, at the north end of the main island. As we have seen, it is the harbour from which we take a boat to visit the Blue Caves.

Pelouzo

Pelouzo, to the north-west of the beach of Yerakas, is a low green islet, almost circular in shape with a diameter of just over 500 m.

Marathonisi

Marathonisi, which lies of the Lake of Keri is a, narrow rocky island, less than a kilometre long and about 250 metres wide.

Myzithres

Finally, mention should be made of two characteristic rocks, rather than islands, which are conical in shape and a feature of considerable natural beauty. They are called Megali Myzithra and Mikri Myzithra, and can be seen from the lighthouse of Keri, or from the sea, when visiting the Cave of Keri.

Aghios Ioannis

The largest of these rocky islets lies off the steep west and south-west coast of the island, at the entrance to the bay of Porto Vromi, some 7 km. away from the village of Anaphonitria. To the south are two more barren islets, **Karanionisi**, south-west of the village of Aghios Nikolaos (or Kiliomeno) and **Kentinaria**, east of Keri.

STROPHADES

a natural and cultural monument

Harpies depicted on the Spartan bowl.

The Strophades, or Strophadia, are two little islets lying in the deep blue waters of the Ionian sea. They are called Megalo Strophadi or Stamphani, and Arpyia. The ancient author Apollonios of Rhodes calls them "the floating islands", because they seem to be floating on the surface of the water. Virgil recounts the legend of the Strophades in his Aenid:

"Zetis and Calais, the children of Boreas (the north wind) and Oreithyia, were pursuing the Harpies... These terrible monsters, daughters of Thaumas and the ocean-nymph Electra, were goddesses of storms and winds... They pursued them as far as the Strophades, but, at Zeus's orders, returned home empty-handed."

The ancient geographer Strabo took over the name Strophades, and wrote of these islands: "Along the coast lie two islands called the Srophades, four hundred stades distant from the mainland, in the Libyan and southern ocean".

In its loneliness, the lighthouse on the island gazes on the few visitors.

Nature & position

Strophadi or Stamphani has an area of 2.5 sq. km and the smaller Arpyia only 1.5 sq. km Strophadi is quadrilateral in shape, and Arpyia quite irregular. They lie 27 nautical miles away from the southernmost point of Zakynthos, and 28 miles from the Peloponnese (Katakolo). The greatest height on Strophadi is 21.92 m. and that on Arpyia 10.60 m. The islands are virtually flat. Their coasts are steep and rocky, and there are no sandy beaches.

The windswept north coast of Megalo Strophadi is covered with low creeping shrub. Since 1887 a lighthouse has stood at the highest point of the island that can be seen for 18 miles. In former times, there were five lighthouse-keepers who lived in the little house next to it. No one lives there now, and the lighthouse is operated by solar energy. In olden times the islands were smothered with vegetation, but the monks reclaimed about 2/3 of Megalo Strophadi to grow the food they needed in order to survive.

In an area of 15 hectares, they grew wheat, barley and oats, as well as garden produce and citrus-trees. The thick grass provided food for a large flock of sheep and goats.

Little of this has survived to meet the scant needs of the only remaining monk. In earlier times there was one of the best orchards in the Mediterranean here, with oranges, lemons, and other citrus-trees. There were 18 wells of crystal-clear water on the island, helping to produce very tasty fruit. Nowadays, the garden of the monk Grigoris grows everything from artichokes to lemons, oranges, figs, almonds and mulberries.

An engraving of the Strophades from the book by Salvator Ludwig (1900).

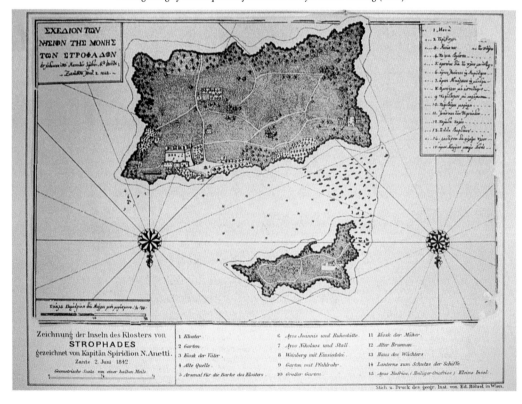

In spring, thousands of birds call here to rest on their journey from Africa. The earliest references to the bird-life of the Strophades date from 1898, when the Austrian ornithologist Otmar Reizer visited the islets for the first time. The names of birds started to become the focus of scientific attention. The great passage of trygonia begins in the middle of April. So far, more than 1220 species of birds have been observed passing over the island during the migrating season. From the evidence at our disposal, it appears that the islands were not visited in the past by botanists (first botanical missions 1992-1997).

Nevertheless, 250 species of plants have been discovered on the island to date. In spring, its meadows are covered with beautiful pink gladioli and other wild flowers. The pyramid orchids, whose flowers are pink to red and arranged in the shape of a pyramid, flowers at this period in shady, damp regions, amidst the low vegetation. Raunculus asiaticus, which is rather like the red poppy, is a rare species and was previously known in Greece only in the south Aegean island arc.

Amongst the daisies in the meadows grow names of flowers, as well as convolvulus asiaticus, a species very rare in Greece, and name, which is thought to be native to Sardinia and Corsica.

Orchidea serapia is another rare variety, found on the other Ionian islands and in some parts of Epiros. It is evident that the Srophades were once smothered with lavish vegetation, some important relics of which survive to the present day. The tall cedars are a dominant feature of this vegetation.

There are very few forests of these trees in Greece, and the Strophades forest is unique, certainly within Greece and possibly throughout the Mediterranean. The forest is so thick that in some places it resembles a jungle; its vegetation consists of a variety of hard-leaf shrubs, such as names. According to tradition, Aghios

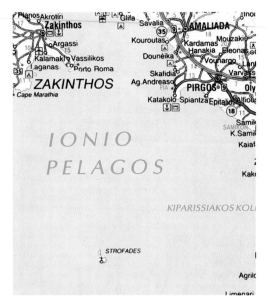

Dionysios spent many hours in this thick forest. He withdrew as a hermit to the cave now known as the Saint's Cave, where he passed his time in prayer. There is a beautiful cross-adorned with shells above the cave, to show passers-by the place where the Saint spent his days in thought and reflection. The dense cedar forest begins at this point, and is so thick that even the sun's rays fail to penetrate it. The thick trunks of the cedars are embraced by dense ivy. The variety of forms seems incredible in so small an island. Different ecosystems are existing side by side and most of the times they leave speechless every visitor that arrives to this part of the earth. The beauty they discover leaves them speechless and determined to come back. The Strophades are also an important port of call for migrating water birds.

An EU guideline calls upon member-states to protect migrating birds. It also forbids the shooting of birds during the nesting period and the various stages of reproduction. This applies to all species.

Despite this, the Sporades are the scene of considerable poaching every year.

The islands are included in the Important Bird Areas list of protected areas for birds of Greece, and are also part of the Kopin programme, as an important biotope.

The cedar forest, the great value of the islands as a calling point for thousands of migrating birds, the rare flora, and their great palaeontological interest have led to the Strophades being declared "natural monuments".

History

In Byzantine times there was a lookout post on the Strophades to keep watch on the sea. According to tradition, an imperial ship was in danger of sinking off the Strophades due to a great storm and the gales that were blowing (1241). The precious cargo of the vessel was Irene, daughter of Theodoros Laskaris, emperor of Nikaia. Irene took refuge on the island and was saved. In gratitude, she built the **monastery of the Panaghia Pantochara** there, which was later renovated by John V Palaiologos. The imposing monastery is one of the jewels of the Greek cultural heritage. An impregnable fortress with canon embrasures for defence against the pirates, it now withstands the strong winds of the Ionian sea and the corrosive effects of time. The finest craftsmen worked hard under the most adverse conditions to build this miracle of architecture, which captivates you from whatever side, you view it.

Monks from monastery Strophadon from the book on Zakynthos by Salvator Ludwig (1900).

With the passage of time, in response to the housing needs of the monks – who at one point were as many as 150 in number – other buildings were added, giving the monastery the form it still has today. Many well-known and anonymous monks withdrew to the Strophades.

Saint Dionysios amongst them. Dionysios died in 1622 on Zakynthos and, in accordance with his wishes, his relic was brought to the monastery on the Strophades where he had been a monk. The old candelabra tremble above the saint's tomb in the chapel of Aghios Georghios. Old Byzantine icons, candelabra, and gold-embroidered fabrics attest to the former brilliance of the imperial monastery on the Strophades. The monastery was frequently the object of pirate attacks. It was plundered in 1716, and the saint's relic was dismembered. The decision was therefore taken to return it to Zakynthos. The double-headed eagle, emblem of authority of the last Byzantine emperors, and especially the Palaeologi, adorns the vestibule. The katholikon (monastery church) is dedicated to the Transfiguration of the Saviour and the Virgin Pantochara, and is a monument of rare beauty and architectural value. Abandonment and the decay of time have left their marks, however. Icons destroyed by the damp, demolished walls, cracks caused by earthquakes.

How much longer will this jewel of the Greek cultural heritage last? This castle of Christendom on the west fringe of Greece has stoutly resisted the barbarian hordes. While there is time, the authorities should ensure that this important monument of the Greek cultural heritage is preserved. The metropolitan see of Zakynthos and the local prefecture also have a sacred duty to work together with the Ministry of Culture in restoring the monastery.

Towards this direction can help the archaeological law passed in 1932 according to which Byzantine buildings until 1945 are protected without having to be declared Archaeological Monuments.

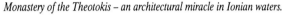

Monastery of the Theotokis – an architectural miracle in Ionian waters.

Bibliography

ARGYRIADOU MARIA, "Ζάκυνθος, όπως την είδα και τη φωτογράφησα", Athens 1976.

VARVIANI N.A., "Η Ζάκυνθος", Athens 1977 (Εθν. Τυπογραφείο).

VOKOTOPOULOS P., "Ζάκυνθος", Αρχ. Δελτίο 24 (1969) Β2, p. 289 - 90.

ZIVAS A. DION., "Η αρχιτεκτνική της Ζακύνθου", Athens 1970.

ZOIS LEONIDAS, "Ιστορία της Ζακύνθου", Athens 1970.

"Λεξικόν ιστορικόν και λαογραφικόν Ζακύνθου", Athens (1970), 1898.

Ιστορικές σελίδες Ζακύνθου, "Αι εν Ζακύνθω Συντεχνίαι", Zakynthos 1893.

KEROFILA K., "Η επτάνησος υπό τους Βενετούς", Athens 1942.

KONOMOU DINOU, "Άγιος Διονύσιος, ο πολιούχος Ζακύνθου", Athens 1969.

Το Ζακυνθινό λαϊκό θέατρο, "Επτανησιακά Φύλλα", Δεκ. 1953, p. 47- 48.

LIVANTHINOΣ A.N., "Le climat de Zante Annales de l'Observatoire Nationale d'Athenes XI" (1930 -1931) 161.

XIROUCHAKIS AGATHAGELOS, "Η Βενετοκρατούμενη Ανατολή, Κρήτη και Επτάνησος", Athens 1934.

"ΠΕΡΙΠΛΟΥΣ", Ζακυνθινό, τριμηνιαίο περιοδικό για τα γράμματα και τις τέχνες, από το 1984, edit. Δ. Βίτσος.

ROMAS DION., "Περίπλους 1570-1870", Athens 1968.

Η πόλη της Ζακύνθου πριν και μετά την ένωση "Χρονικά Ζακύνθου" vol. A', 1964 p. 153 -175.

SALVATOR LUDWING, "Zante", 2 vol., Prag 1904

SIMOPOULOS KYR., "Ξένοι ταξιδιώτες στην Ελλάδα", vol. A, B, Γ, Athens 1981.

GREEK COOKERY & Wines

Avaible in 12 languages

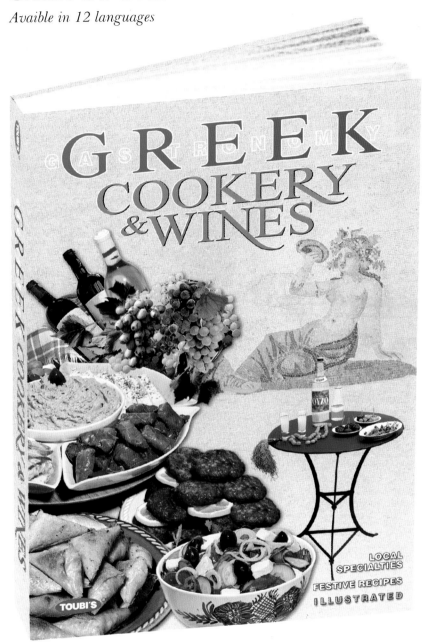

A luxury edition which takes us into the magical world of Greek cuisine with traditional recipes, local specialities, pastries, wines and other beverages, from all the areas of Greece and Cyprus, each recipe with the estimated number of calories. 170 colour photographs, pages: 192, format: 17 × 24